THE VEGETABLE YEAR COOKBOOK

Judy Ridgway

Futura

A Futura Book

Copyright © 1985 Judy Ridgway

First published in Great Britain in 1985
by Judy Piatkus (Publishers) Ltd, London

This edition published in 1986 by
Futura Publications, a Division of
Macdonald and Co (Publishers) Ltd
London & Sydney

ISBN 0 7088 3126 5

Printed in Great Britain by The Guernsey Press

Futura Publications
A Division of
Macdonald & Co (Publishers) Ltd
Greater London House
Hampstead Road
London NW1 7QX

A BPCC plc Company

CONTENTS

INTRODUCTION

Vegetables have been one of my favourite foods for as long as I can remember. My father has always been an extremely keen gardener and our family dinner table was often the testing ground for his latest enthusiasm. Kohlrabi was a commonplace vegetable to us twenty years ago and sugar peas were a family favourite long before we learnt their French name. Vegetables were never over-cooked and even cabbage came crunchy to our table. My parents view with some surprise the modern exhortation to eat more vegetables!

The range of vegetables available in the greengrocers and super-markets nowadays has widened almost beyond recognition, and many of the vegetables which could only be enjoyed abroad or at the table of keen gardeners are now on general sale. Modern transportation methods have brought about a vegetable revolution in the shops just at the time when nutritionists are urging us to change our eating patterns in favour of a higher vegetable intake.

With the exception of certain classic vegetable dishes, such as Cauliflower Cheese, Braised Celery and Stuffed Marrow, vegetables were steamed or baked if they were lucky — and boiled to death if they were not. Foreign travel has broadened the general base, but vegetable cookery still tends to be rather boring.

Of course, perfectly cooked spring vegetables are delicious served on their own or with a little butter, but if we are really to use more vegetables in our diet, we will need to be more adventurous with them. This book is really a response to that need. In it I have tried to create a variety of dishes which use a vegetable as the 'star' ingredient. Some recipes also use meat or fish. Others use only vegetables or vegetables with nuts or dairy produce.

The inspiration for the recipes came from a variety of sources including restaurants here and abroad, old cookery books and the favourite recipes of my friends. I have deliberately omitted the obvious classics on the basis that there will be recipes for them in most other general cookbooks. Sometimes an outline guide to their preparation is given in the introduction to the particular vegetable, and at other times I have adapted the recipe to use a different, sometimes surprising, but still appropriate, vegetable.

As well as recipe ideas I have included some practical advice on dealing with each vegetable and cooking it in a simple fashion, along with a few historical titbits. The fifty-odd vegetables are arranged according to the months of the year. It is easy to forget that there is such a thing as seasonal availability when one sees the large supermarket shelves groaning under the weight of every possible kind of fruit and vegetable. There may be 'winter' home-grown vegetables sitting side by side with vegetables from the tropics or 'summer' vegetables which have come from the other side of the world. Nevertheless, those French beans from abroad will cost a good deal more than the home-grown ones will in the summer. The world may be a provision house for the wealthier countries but economics still rule.

Accordingly, I have decided to place most of the vegetables in the month in which they are most plentiful in the northern hemisphere. In some instances I have chosen the month with which the vegetable is traditionally associated, in others the month in which the home-grown varieties first appear.

Each vegetable has its own requirements when it comes to getting the best out of it, but I think there are three golden rules which apply to the treatment of all vegetables:

* Buy vegetables as fresh as you possibly can.
* Use vegetables as quickly as possible after purchase.
* Cook vegetables as lightly as possible.

Finally, after the title of each recipe, an initial letter in a box indicates how the recipe can be used: as a soup or starter [S] as an accompaniment [A] or as a main course [M]. Each recipe serves four people unless otherwise stated.

JANUARY

'To everything there is a season, and a time to every purpose under the heaven.'

Ecclesiastes 3.1

Celery
Kale
Carrots
Chinese Leaves

CELERY

Celery is one of the most versatile of the winter vegetables. It can be eaten raw with cheese or in salads; it makes an excellent flavouring in soups and stews, and in addition to being cooked and served as an accompaniment to the main dish, it can also be used to make unusual dishes in its own right.

Celery is rich in the B group of vitamins and in minerals such as sodium and potassium. Celery salt is made from the ground seeds, and folk medicine has it that celery is particularly good for rheumatism.

The Romans used celery in some quantity, and as well as eating it themselves they are reputed to have given it to their poultry to eat before slaughtering them for consumption. Celery was felt to give the poultry flesh a very special and desirable flavour! Despite its culinary history, celery was not cultivated in any quantity in the UK until the eighteenth century, though it is derived from a native plant known as 'smallage' which appears among the list of pot herbs in Elizabethan cookery.

Availability: Almost all the year round, though scarcer during the period March to July. Celery is said to be crisper and tastier after the first frosts of winter.

Buying Guide: Choose heads with thick, smooth stalks. They should be fat at the base with pale green leaves. Avoid those with the leaves removed, they could be old.

Storage: Keep in the salad drawer of the fridge. If celery gets limp, stand up to the neck in water.

Preparation: Cut off the root base and remove damaged stalks. Scrub the stalks in cold water. Cut off large leaves and use in soup.

Basic Cooking: Steam sliced stalks for 20—30 minutes. Avoid boiling as this takes away flavour. Serve with butter and herbs or with a cheese sauce. Alternatively braise whole heads or large stalks in a little stock or wine. Use also in stir-fry mixtures and casseroles. Stuff raw sticks with cheese mixtures to make cocktail canapés.

CELERY AND APPLE SALAD [S]

This variation on the standard American Waldorf salad may be served as a starter to a substantial main course or it may be served as part of a salad buffet. Walnuts or cashew nuts could be used in place of hazelnuts.

4 large sticks celery, trimmed and finely chopped
2 small green eating apples, cored and chopped
½ red pepper, seeded and finely chopped
1 oz/25 g hazelnuts, chopped
a very little lemon rind
juice of ½ lemon
1½ tablespoons mayonnaise
1½ tablespoons soured cream or yogurt
salt and pepper
shredded lettuce to serve

Toss the celery, apple, pepper and hazelnuts with the lemon rind and juice. Mix the mayonnaise and soured cream or yogurt to a smooth paste and fold into the salad. Season to taste, and pile up on a bed of lettuce. Serve at once.

CREAM-GLAZED CELERY [S]

This French cream and egg yolk sauce is much quicker to make than a white roux sauce, and it also gives a gourmet touch to an everyday vegetable.

2 heads celery
salt
8 fl. oz/225 ml whipping cream
3 egg yolks
1 tablespoon flaked almonds

Trim the heads of celery of all the leaves and the tough outside stalks. Poach in a little salted water for about 30 minutes until thoroughly tender. Drain well, retaining the cooking liquor, and keep warm.

Boil up the cooking liquor and reduce to about 2 fl. oz/50 ml. Leave to cool. Lightly whisk the cream and beat in the egg yolks. Stir in the celery juice.

Slice the heads of celery and carefully arrange the slices in four individual heatproof dishes. Spread some of the cream mixture over each plate and sprinkle with flaked almonds. Place under a very hot grill and leave for about a minute until the glaze has turned an even golden brown.

CELERY CHEESE [M]

I serve this unusual celery recipe as a lunch or supper dish.

1 small head celery
2 tablespoons milk
6 oz/175 g Cheddar cheese, grated
2 eggs, beaten
celery salt
black pepper
2 oz/50 g fresh wholemeal breadcrumbs

Wash the celery and grate on a medium grater. Place in a saucepan with the milk. Bring to the boil and simmer gently for about 15–20 minutes until the celery is tender. Stir from time to time.

Leave to cool and mix with the cheese, eggs, celery salt and black pepper. Spoon into a greased pie dish and cover with breadcrumbs. Bake at 190°C/375°F/Gas 5 for 30–35 minutes until brown on top.

CELERY WITH PROVENCE DRESSING [A]

This dish is equally good served hot or cold. For the cold version simply add a tablespoonful of lemon juice or cider vinegar.

1 head celery, trimmed and sliced
1 onion, finely sliced
1 tablespoon cooking oil
1 tomato, peeled, seeded and chopped (optional)
1 tablespoon tomato purée
¼ teaspoon fennel seeds
2 sprigs fresh rosemary or ¼ teaspoon dried
2 sprigs fresh thyme or ¼ teaspoon dried
salt and freshly ground black pepper

Steam the celery in a steamer or in a very little salted boiling water until tender. This will take about 20–30 minutes depending on the size and age of the celery.

Meanwhile gently fry the onion in the cooking oil until it turns transparent. Add the tomato and tomato purée and all the herbs and seasoning. Continue cooking gently for about 8—10 minutes, add a little water if the mixture shows signs of getting too dry.

When the celery is cooked, drain well and mix with the Provence dressing and serve or leave to cool.

KALE

This very dark green, crinkly and curly-leafed vegetable is sometimes known as 'borecole'. This is an anglicised version of its Dutch name 'boerenkool' or peasants' cabbage. It is one of the earliest English vegetables and often appeared on Anglo-Saxon tables.

Kale has always been popular with country people and sells better in Scotland than it does in England, where you may have to search about for it. It does have a fairly strong flavour and if you are not sure whether or not the family will like it, try mixing it with white cabbage. This results in a much milder flavour.

Do not confuse kale with seakale, which is quite a different vegetable. Seakale is found growing wild on parts of the English and Irish coasts and is rarely offered for sale in the shops. It is the white stalks rather than the silvery green leaves which are deemed the speciality.

Availability: November to May.

Buying Guide: Choose young-looking leaves which are dark green and fresh. Avoid any which show signs of yellowing.

Storage: Store in a cool place and eat as soon after purchase as possible.

Preparation: Separate the leaves from the stems and cut out the centre rib which may be tough. Wash thoroughly in cold water.

Basic Cooking: Boil or steam in a very little water for 8—10 minutes, taking care not to overcook or the vegetables will go mushy. Alternatively, deep-fry in hot cooking oil or par-boil and then drain and cook with diced bacon.

SPECIAL TIP. Kale is a fairly coarse-leafed vegetable and needs to be very finely shredded before using in salads or in cooking. Prepare at the last minute to retain maximum vitamin C.

KALE SALAD [A]

Yogurt or quark low-fat soft cheese can easily be substituted for the soured cream in this recipe.

8 oz/225g curly kale, very finely shredded
2 sticks celery, very finely sliced
2 tablespoons flaked almonds or chopped salted peanuts
1 tablespoon raisins
3 tablespoons soured cream
salt and black pepper

Toss all the ingredients in a bowl just before serving. Leave out the salt if using salted peanuts.

KALE WITH SPICED PEAS [A]

I find that the strong flavour of the kale blends well with the curry on the peas. Add more yogurt if the flavours are too robust for your palate.

3 tablespoons cooking oil
2 teaspoons whole cumin seeds
2 bay leaves
8 oz/225 g frozen peas
½ teaspoon curry powder
½ teaspoon turmeric
3 fl. oz/75 ml stock
1 lb/450 g curly kale, stalks removed, shredded
2 tablespoons plain yogurt
salt and pepper

Heat the cooking oil in a pan and fry the cumin seeds and bay leaves for ½ minute. Add the peas, curry powder, turmeric and stock. Bring to the boil and simmer for 8 minutes.

Meanwhile steam the kale in a steamer or in a very little boiling salted water until almost tender. Drain well and add to the peas. Stir and continue cooking until the kale is fully cooked. Stir in the yogurt and season to taste.

FRIED KALE WITH ALMONDS [A]

Treated in this way curly kale tastes just like Chinese deep-fried seaweed. Serve it as a starter as part of a Chinese meal or as an accompaniment with other vegetables.

5—6 oz/150—175 g curly kale
2 tablespoons flaked almonds
cooking oil

Remove the stalks and shred the curly kale finely. Mix with the flaked almonds. Pour about ½ in/1 cm of cooking oil into the bottom of a large heavy based pan. Heat until very hot. Drop half the kale mixture into the pan and stir. Take care as the fat will splash a little.

When all the kale is crispy — this happens very quickly — remove with a slotted spoon and place on kitchen paper to drain. Repeat the process with the remaining kale mixture. Drain and serve at once.

CARROTS

Like kale, carrots were very popular in medieval times and they have remained firm favourites ever since. Their introduction to the UK is variously credited to the Flemings and to the Romans before them. Certainly the Romans used plenty of carrots and in his Roman cookery book Apicius gave recipes for fried carrots and for carrots with parsnips. Carrots are, of course, grown for their roots but the court ladies in the time of Charles I wore the pretty foliage as a decoration.

Carrots are rich in Vitamin A, a deficiency of which leads to night blindness. Hence the exhortations during the last war to eat plenty of carrots to help cope with the black-out! Carrots also contain quite a lot of sugar and this quality was particularly useful to cooks who did not have the benefit of sugar-cane. Christmas pudding recipes often list grated carrots among the ingredients — for sweetening and moisture — and in America carrot cake has remained a classic.

Availability: All the year round.

Buying Guide: In the spring young carrots are sold in bunches usually with the foliage attached. These have a particularly good flavour. All carrots should be well shaped and smooth skinned with a good colour. Watch out for worm holes and mechanical damage.

Storage: Keep in a cool, dark, airy place. For longer storage choose unwashed carrots.

Preparation: Top and tail all carrots and then scrub or scape young carrots and peel old ones. Cook whole or sliced. Grate for use in salads.

Basic Cooking: Boil or steam until just tender. Toss in butter or cream, or flavour with herbs or orange rind. Alternatively serve in a sauce. Roast in foil or round the joint. Use in soups and casseroles. For glazed or Vichy carrots, boil with a knob of butter, a teaspoon of sugar and plenty of salt and pepper. Boil fast until all the liquid has disappeared.

GLAZED CARROTS WITH ONIONS   [A]

This simple variation of the classic glazed or Vichy carrots is much more interesting than the original. Serve with any roast or grilled meat.

12 oz/350 g carrots, peeled and sliced
2 onions, coarsely chopped
½ oz/15 g butter
salt and freshly ground black pepper

Place the carrots and onions in a saucepan and just cover with water. Add the butter and the seasonings. Bring to the boil and boil until all the liqued has evaporated and the carrots are tender.

CARROTS WITH CELERY

Carrots and celery are two winter standbys, and I came across the combination in a restaurant tucked away in the Yorkshire Dales.

12 oz/350 g carrots, diced
½ oz/15 g butter

6 large sticks celery, diced
1 onion, chopped
½ teaspoon caraway seeds
1 teaspoon plain flour
½ teaspoon sugar
1 tablespoon white wine or cider
salt and pepper

Cook the carrots in lightly salted boiling water until tender. Drain well.

Melt the butter in a pan and gently fry the celery, onion and caraway seeds for about 8—10 minutes, stirring from time to time. The vegetables are ready when the celery is soft and the onion is lightly browned.

Add the carrots and the remaining ingredients and stir over a medium heat until the carrots are heated through.

CARROTS WITH ORANGE [A]

Orange seems to bring out the best in carrots, and there are classic soups and salads using the two ingredients. I have used the same idea for a very quick and simple vegetable dish. Serve with grilled steaks.

1¼ lb/575 g carrots, peeled and chopped
1 tablespoon cream
½ oz/15 g butter
½ teaspoon grated orange rind
salt and black pepper

Cook the carrots in lightly salted water for 15 minutes until really tender.

Mash well and mix with all the other ingredients. Beat well over a low heat.

CARROT AND FENNEL COLESLAW [A]

Cabbage is of course the usual base for coleslaw but there is really no reason why other vegetables should not be pressed into service. Here's an idea I worked out while in France one summer. I experimented with lovely long thin new carrots, but any carrots will do.

3 carrots, peeled and cut into long thin sticks
1 small head Italian fennel, very finely sliced

3 tablespoons mayonnaise
½ teaspoon made mustard (optional)
black pepper

Blanch the carrot and fennel for 3 minutes in boiling water. Plunge into cold water for the same time. Drain very well and leave to cool.

Mix with mayonnaise, mustard if used, and season to taste. Keep in the fridge until required.

COLD CARROT SALAD [A]

This is a useful recipe for using up leftover cooked carrots but it is also good enough to cook the carrots specially.

8 oz/225 g baby carrots, peeled or scraped
3 tablespoons olive oil
juice of 1 lemon
a little grated lemon rind
1—2 cloves of garlic, to taste, crushed
1½ tablespoons freshly chopped parsley
¼ teaspoon whole cumin seeds
½ teaspoon paprika pepper

Steam the carrots in a steamer or in a very little boiling salted water for 15—20 minutes until just tender. Drain well.

Meanwhile mix all the remaining ingredients and chill in the fridge. Pour over the carrots while still warm. Cool and keep in the fridge until required.

CARROT KUGEL

This traditional Jewish dish is served as a dessert. It makes a very good family pudding in the cold winter months.

8 oz/225 g carrots
1 oz/25 g butter
1 oz/25 g plain flour
1 oz/25 g cornflour
1 small cooking apple
juice and grated rind of 1 lemon
2 tablespoons sherry
4 oz/100 g sugar
4 eggs, separated

Peel and grate the carrots and sweat in the butter until soft. Add the flours to the butter and carrots and stir to a smoothish paste. Remove from the heat.

Peel, core and grate the apple. Add to carrot mixture with the grated rind and juice of the lemon, sherry and sugar. Beat egg yolks into the mixture.

Whisk egg whites to medium peaks and stir a small amount of egg white into the mixture. Fold in the remaining egg white very carefully. Bake in a preheated oven at 190°C/375°F/ Gas 5 for 40 minutes. Serve immediately.

CARROT CAKE

This recipe together with its cream cheese icing comes straight from a friend in Washington DC. It is quite large and will serve 8–10 people.

1 lb/450 g plain flour
2 teaspoons baking powder
2 teaspoons bicarbonate of soda
2 teaspoons ground cinnamon
½ teaspoon salt
12 oz/350 g sugar
1 teaspoon vanilla essence
½ pint/300 ml vegetable oil
1 lb/450 g raw carrots, grated
4 eggs
1 oz/25 g ground almonds
1 oz/25 g chopped walnuts

Frosting
3 oz/75 g cream cheese
2 oz/50 g butter
9 oz/250 g icing sugar
1 teaspoon lemon juice

Sift the flour, baking powder, bicarbonate of soda, cinnamon and salt into a bowl. In another bowl mix the sugar, vanilla essence, vegetable oil and carrots. Blend the latter mixture thoroughly, then add the eggs, one at a time, beating well after each addition. Fold in the flour mixture and the nuts. Spoon into a loose-based 8 inch/20 cm cake tin and bake at 180°C/350°F/Gas 4 for about an hour until cooked through. Test with a skewer and leave to cool.

When the cake is cold mix together all the frosting ingredients. Cut the cake in half and use a third of the frosting to fill the cake. Replace the top and spread the rest of the frosting all over the cake. Mark all over with a fork to decorate.

NB Don't worry about the vast quantity of oil in this recipe. It may not be very healthy, but it keeps the cake deliciously moist.

SPECIAL TIP. To make a carrot purée, boil roughly chopped carrots in a little boiling salted water until tender. Drain well and purée in a blender or food processor. Mix with a little butter and cream and season to taste. If you like, add a tablespoon of roughly chopped blanched almonds. Shape into individual portions with two tablespoons.

This works equally well with other vegetables. To swedes, you could add a pinch of grated nutmeg and a little grated lemon rind; to parsnip purée, a few toasted pine kernels, roughly chopped; to sprouts half a teaspoon of coriander seeds, coarsely ground.

CHINESE LEAVES

This vegetable, which looks a little like a paler and slightly over-grown Cos lettuce, is a recent introduction to the UK market, but it is growing in popularity. It can be eaten raw in salads or it can be shredded and cooked as a vegetable.

Sometimes also known as Chinese Cabbage, this vegetable is popular in the East and is often served in Chinese restaurants in Won Ton Soup or as Chinese greens.

Availability: All the year round.

Buying Guide: Look for crisp, fresh samples. Usually sold by weight, retailers will often sell halves or even quarters.

Storage: Wash and dry the leaves and store in a polythene bag in the salad compartment of the fridge or in a cold larder for up to a week.

Preparation: Wash in cold water and dry. Eat or cook leaves whole or shredded.

Basic Cooking: Cook in a very little boiling salted water. Do not overcook, for Chinese leaves should still be crisp after cooking. Alternatively stir-fry with nuts, vegetables or meats; stuff and bake the larger leaves or braise with tomatoes.

CHINESE LEAVES PEKING-STYLE [M]

Not surprisingly, Chinese leaves really lend themselves to the Chinese style of cooking.

1 lb/450 g lean pork, minced
4 spring onions, minced
2 teaspoons fresh root ginger, grated
salt and pepper
1 tablespoon cooking oil
2 tablespoons soy sauce
1 onion, sliced
1 green pepper, seeded and sliced
1 tablespoon chicken stock or water
1 lb/450 g Chinese leaves, thinly sliced

Mix the pork with the spring onions, ginger and seasoning and form into about forty small balls. Heat the cooking oil in a wok or large frying pan and fry the meatballs all over for about 6—7 minutes until they are cooked through. Remove from the pan and keep on one side.

Add the soy sauce to the pan with the onion and green pepper. Stir-fry, keeping the vegetables on the move, for 1 minute. Next add the stock and Chinese leaves and continue stir-frying for a further minute. Return the meatballs to the pan and toss everything together to heat through. Serve with rice or noodles.

STUFFED CHINESE LEAVES [M]

This recipe was inspired by a Polish recipe for stuffed cabbage, and the ingredients seem to go equally well with the rather stronger flavour of the Chinese leaves.

1 head Chinese leaves
2 oz/50 g uncooked long-grain rice
3 tomatoes, peeled and chopped
2 oz/50 g chopped mixed nuts (almonds, hazelnuts, walnuts)
1 onion, finely chopped

3 tablespoons freshly chopped parsley
salt and pepper
1 chicken stock cube
1 pint/600 ml boiling water
juice of 1 lemon

Remove twelve of the large outer leaves and blanch by plunging into boiling water for 1 minute. Transfer to a bowl of cold water and drain. Mix the rice, tomatoes, nuts, onion and parsley in a bowl and season.

Place a tablespoon of the filling on each Chinese leaf and roll up neatly, taking care not to tear it.

Shred the remaining Chineses leaves and place in the base of a wide saucepan. Carefully arrange the stuffed leaves on top. Mix the stock cube with the boiling water and pour over the top. Pour on the lemon juice and bring to the boil. Simmer gently for 30 minutes.

CHINESE SHREDDED SALAD [M]

I have used some of the flavours of the classic Chinese cuisine for this all-in-one salad. Add a good potato salad to complete the meal.

½ small or ¼ large head Chinese leaves, finely shredded
¼ green pepper, seeded and cut into thin strips
2 oz/50 g beansprouts
4 oz/100 g cooked ham, cut into strips
4 oz/100g cooked chicken meat or tongue, cut into strips
2 oz/50 g Tilsit or Gouda cheese, sliced and cut into strips
pinch five-spice powder
juice of 1 lemon
1 teaspoon soy sauce
1 tablespoon oil
salt and plenty of black pepper

Toss all the vegetables together and then add the meat and cheese strips. Sprinkle with a little five-spice powder.

Mix all the remaining ingredients and pour over the top. Serve at once.

CHINESE LEAVES BAKED A LA LORRAINE [A]

This recipe originally developed for white cabbage is equally good with the Chinese variety. Serve with plain roasts and grills.

1 small or ½ large head Chinese leaves, cut into 4 pieces
1 small onion, sliced
1 oz/25 g butter
2 tomatoes, peeled and chopped
large pinch caraway seeds
½ oz/15 g flour
½ pint/300 ml vegetable stock or water
salt and pepper
3 tablespoons soured cream
1 tablespoon chopped parsley

Blanch the Chinese leaves in lightly salted boiling water for 7—8 minutes. Place in a casserole.

Fry the onion in the butter until very lightly browned. Add the tomatoes and continue frying for a minute or so. Stir in the caraway seeds, flour and then the stock. Continue cooking and stirring until the mixture thickens, then add the seasonings and pour over the leaves in the casserole.

Bake at 180°C/350°F/Gas 4 for an hour, basting occasionally. Pour the soured cream over the top, 15 minutes before the end of the cooking time, and sprinkle with parsley just before serving.

CHINESE LEAVES WITH BACON [A]

Take care not to overcook the Chinese leaves in this recipe. They are much nicer if quite crunchy. I particularly like to serve the dish with quickly sautéed liver.

4 oz/100 g smoked bacon, diced
1 onion, finely chopped
12 oz/350 g Chinese leaves, sliced
freshly ground black pepper
pinch caraway seeds

Fry the diced bacon in a non-stick pan to release some of the fat, then add the onion. Continue frying for 3—4 minutes until the onion begins to soften.

Add all the remaining ingredients and cook over a medium heat, stirring all the time, for a further 3 or 4 minutes until the leaves start to soften. Serve at once.

SPECIAL TIP. Chinese leaves are exceptionally good cooked with juniper berries. Allow a teaspoon of juniper berries to one head of Chinese leaves and use in boiled, steamed or stir-fry dishes.

FEBRUARY

'The discovery of a new dish does more for the
happiness of mankind than the discovery of a stew.'

Jean Anthelme Brillat-Savarin (1825)

Leeks
Parsnips
Mushrooms
Avocados

LEEKS

The use of the leek as a Welsh emblem is said to date back to AD 640 when the Welsh fought a successful battle against the Saxons. The Welsh wore leeks in their hats to distinguish them from the enemy. However, the leek is not only a traditional Welsh insignia, it is also a useful winter vegetable. It has a milder, sweeter flavour than onion but nevertheless a predominating one.

Leeks are often used in soups; particularly the traditional Welsh cauls and in Vichyssoise, the classic French soup. In the Middle East they are used in hors d'oeuvres with black olives. The Romans used them raw in salads and this is well worth trying today. The Romans added a peppery sauce, and a vinaigrette with a few green peppercorns will reproduce the dish quite well.

Availability: August to May

Buying Guide: Choose straight, well shaped leeks which have been trimmed of their greenery. Avoid those which have been too closely trimmed at the root end or which have yellow or discoloured leaves.

Storage: Keep in a cool, dark, airy place or in the salad compartment of the fridge for a few days.

Preparation: Remove tough outer leaves and take care to remove all dirt from between the leaves. Leave whole or slice into lengths or rings. Finely chop to eat raw.

Basic Cooking: Leeks can be boiled or steamed and served with a white or cheese sauce. They may also be braised on top of the stove or sliced and baked in the oven with a little butter or stock and, for a more unusual flavour, a sprig of mint. Use also in soups, stews and casseroles. Cold cooked leeks with a vinaigrette sauce and a little sliced onion make an excellent starter. Leeks shrink substantially on cooking and this should be allowed for in estimating quantities.

LEEK AND POTATO SOUP

A warming soup that is simple to make, but with the addition of cream and a pretty garnish is turned into something quite special. Add croutons if liked.

12 oz/350 g potatoes, peeled and chopped
1 large onion, finely chopped
2 large leeks, cleaned and roughly chopped
1 clove garlic, crushed
2 oz/50 g butter
1½ pints/850 ml chicken stock
¼ pint/150 ml double cream
salt and pepper
2 tablespoons chopped parsley
fine matchstick strips of leek to garnish

In a large saucepan fry the potatoes, onion, leeks and garlic in the butter for 8–10 minutes. This should be done slowly so that the vegetables do not brown. Add the chicken stock and bring to the boil. Simmer gently for about 20–25 minutes until the vegetables are tender.

Either sieve or liquidise the soup. Return to a clean pan and add the cream, salt and pepper to taste, and the parsley. Stir over a gentle heat until hot.

Sprinkle with strips of leek and serve.

CORNISH 'LIKKY' PIE   [M]

This is an adaptation of the extremely rich original recipe which used Cornish clotted cream and had a pastry topping. The latter can still be added when the eggs and cream go in.

1½ lb/700 g potatoes, peeled and sliced
2 lb/1 kg leeks, trimmed and sliced
8 oz/225 g lean bacon rashers, cut into pieces
2 large eggs, beaten
¼ pint/150 ml soured cream
3 fl. oz/75 ml milk
salt and pepper
shortcrust pastry (optional)

Layer the potatoes, leeks and bacon in a large pie dish. Cover with a lid or with foil and bake at 190°C/375°F/Gas 5 for 20 minutes.

Mix the eggs with the soured cream, milk and seasoning and pour over the vegetables. Top with a pastry crust if desired or cover with the lid. Continue baking for 40–45 minutes until the pastry and the potatoes are cooked through.

FRIED LEEK PUFFS [A]

These cheesy puffs can also make a good starter served with a little tomato sauce.

1 lb/450g leeks, cleaned and very finely chopped
1 oz/25 g butter
1 lb/450g potatoes
salt
2 oz/50g Parmesan cheese, grated
1 egg, beaten
¼ teaspoon curry powder
cooking oil

Gently fry the leeks in butter until soft and very lightly brown. Boil the potatoes in salted water. Peel and mash. Stir the leeks and cheese into the mashed potato, and beat in the egg and curry powder.

Heat the fat in a saucepan and drop spoonfuls of the mixture into the fat. Turn over to fry each side and remove when golden all over. Fry the mixture in batches of three to four, and keep warm until all the mixture has been used up.

BRAISED LEEKS IN WHITE WINE SAUCE [A]

All too often leeks in white sauce end up rather tasteless. This method, however, ensures plenty of flavour.

1½ lb/700 g leeks, trimmed and cleaned
4 fl oz/100 ml dry white wine
salt and pepper
¾ oz/20 g butter
¾ oz/ 20 g plain flour
¼ pint/150 ml half and half milk and water
2 oz/50 g Emmenthal or Cheddar cheese, grated
pinch grated nutmeg

Slice the leeks and arrange in a shallow ovenproof dish. Pour the wine over the top and sprinkle with seasonings. Cover with foil and bake at 200°C/400°F/Gas 6 for about 40 minutes until tender.

Melt the butter in a pan and stir in the flour. Gradually add the liquid from the leeks, and the milk and water. Bring to the boil, stirring all the time. Cook for 3 minutes, add the cheese and nutmeg and season to taste. Pour over the leeks and return to the oven for a further 15 minutes.

LEEK AND HAM AU GRATIN [M]

As a variation of the above, steam the leeks for 5—8 minutes in a little boiling salted water. Drain and wrap each leek in a slice of ham. Make the liquid up to ¼ pint/150 ml with milk and continue as for white wine sauce.

Arrange the leeks and ham in a shallow heatproof dish, pour on the sauce and top with extra cheese. Finish off under the grill.

LEEKS WITH PEAS [A]

This recipe goes particularly well with grilled or fried liver, or with fish.

3 rashers streaky bacon, diced
½ oz/15 g butter
2 lb/1 kg leeks, trimmed and finely chopped
8 oz/225 g frozen peas
¼ teaspoon dried savory
salt and black pepper

Gently fry the bacon in the butter for 2—3 minutes. Add the leeks and continue frying gently until the leeks are tender. This takes about 8—10 minutes. Stir from time to time and do not allow the leeks to brown.

Cook the peas in the normal way. Drain and mix with the leeks and bacon, adding the savory and seasoning to taste.

PARSNIPS

Parsnips are native to Britain and were the traditional accompaniment to roast beef before potatoes were introduced. They have been cultivated for centuries, and are unusual in that in their wild or uncultivated state they were inedible. No one knows how early farmers came to develop the cultivated varieties.

Parsnips, like carrots, are a sweet vegetable and this sweetness is retained to a much greater degree if they are not boiled. The sweetness can also be used to good effect in home wine-making, and parsnip wine is said to be one of the very best of the root vegetable wines. Some eighteenth-century writers believed that a good parsnip wine could rival Malmsey or Canary.

Availability: August to April.

Buying Guide: Avoid those with soft brown patches on the shoulders. Buy unwashed vegetables to last longer.

Storage: Keep in a cool, dry, airy place for several days.

Preparation: Thinly peel all parsnips and quarter old ones to cut out the hard woody core. Grate raw parsnips for salads.

Basic Cooking: Boil or steam for 40 minutes whole, 35 minutes sliced or 30 minutes diced, and serve with butter and parsley. Or mash with butter and seasonings or with other vegetables such as potatoes or carrots and marrow. Parsnips can also be par-boiled and fried, roasted in foil or with the joint. Cut into thin sticks and deep-fry to make parsnip chips. Use also in soups and casseroles.

CURRIED PARSNIP SOUP   [S]

Almost any root vegetable except perhaps beetroot can be substituted for parsnips in this recipe.

1 large onion, sliced
1 tablespoon cooking oil
knob of butter
1 lb/450 g parsnips, peeled and chopped
1 tablespoon curry powder
salt and black pepper
1½ pints/900 ml chicken stock

Fry the onion in the cooking oil and butter in a large saucepan until lightly browned. Add the parsnips and curry powder and continue frying for 2–3 minutes. Add the seasonings and stock and bring to the boil. Simmer for 30 minutes until the parsnips are tender.

Purée or sieve, and reheat before serving.

PARSNIP TORTILLA [M]

This recipe is developed from a similar recipe using potatoes alone. However I think that the sweetness of the parsnips really enhances the flavour of the dish.

12 oz/350 g potatoes, peeled and grated
12 oz/350 g parsnips, peeled and grated
1 large onion, very finely chopped
3 eggs, beaten
princh dried marjoram
salt and pepper
2 tablespoons cooking oil

Strain any liquid from the vegetables and mix together with the eggs, herb and seasonings.

Heat the cooking oil in a frying pan and add the potato and parsnip mixture. Press down into a 'cake' shape. Reduce the heat and cook for about 10–15 minutes until the base is well browned. Turn over and cook on the second side for a further 10 minutes.

PARSNIP RÉMOULADE [A]

Celeriac is the usual ingredient of the classic dish made in this way, but parsnips stand up equally well to the treatment.

12 oz/350 g parsnips, peeled and cut into thin sticks
3 tablespoons mayonnaise
1 teaspoon made mustard (optional)
salt and pepper

Cook the parsnip sticks in lightly salted boiling water for 15 minutes so that they are still fairly crunchy. Drain and leave to cool.

Mix all the remaining ingredients and toss the cold parsnip sticks in this mixture. Chill for 30 minutes or so before serving.

PARSNIP AND PARSLEY CROQUETTES [A]

Serve these delicious croquettes — the mixture makes eight — with grilled lamb chops or with grilled fish.

1½ lb/700 g parsnips, peeled and sliced
salt
2 oz/50 g butter
2 tablespoons freshly chopped parsley
plenty of black pepper
fresh breadcrumbs
1 large egg, beaten
cooking oil

Cook the parsnips in plenty of salted boiling water for about 20 minutes or until tender. Drain very well and beat in the butter, parsley and black pepper.

Leave to cool a little then shape into sausage-shaped croquettes. Roll in breadcrumbs, then in beaten egg and then again in breadcrumbs, making sure they are well covered. Deep-fry in hot cooking oil for 3 minutes or shallow-fry on all sides.

MUSHROOMS

At one time the only mushrooms available were the field mushrooms which sprouted up in the autumn fields. Country people would get up early in the morning to pick the mushrooms for breakfast or perhaps to sell at the local market. Nowadays these field mushrooms are quite hard to find, and in the UK mushrooms mean cultivated button, cap or open mushrooms.

Some oyster mushrooms which are both milder and larger are beginning to appear in the shops. But if you want to try the many continental mushrooms such as cèpes and morels you may have to buy dried or canned.

Availability: All the year round.

Buying Guide: For freshness look for a firm cap and fleshy stem. Remember that the larger open mushrooms will have a stronger flavour than buttons, and they also tend to impart a darker colour to any dish in which they are used.

Storage: Place the punnet or bag in which they were bought in a polythene bag and keep in a cool place. Keep in the fridge for up to a week but do not wash before storage. If mushrooms do dry out before use revive by immersing in boiling water for a minute. Dry and use.

Preparation: There is no need to peel mushrooms unless the skins have dried out. Simply wash and use whole, sliced or chopped. Eat raw or cooked.

Basic Cooking: Quickly fry or grill whole mushrooms in butter or sauté sliced mushrooms with a little onion or garlic and parsley. Use whole or sliced in soups and casseroles or as a garnish for other dishes. Chop and use in sauces and stuffings.

CRAB-STUFFED MUSHROOMS [S]

Crab makes a real change from the usual mushroom stuffings. Serve these baked mushrooms as a starter or stuff smaller button mushrooms and serve as part of a cocktail buffet.

1 x 7½ oz/215 g can white crabmeat
3 spring onions, finely chopped
1 oz/25 g Parmesan cheese, grated
1 tablespoon mayonnaise
salt and pepper
12 mushroom caps, stalks removed
knob of butter

Drain the crabmeat well and remove any cartilage. Mix the crabmeat with the spring onions, most of the cheese and the mayonnaise. Season to taste.

   Lightly fry the mushroom caps in the butter and fill with the crab mixture. Place in a shallow dish and bake at 180°C/350°F/Gas 4 for 5 minutes. Sprinkle with the remaining cheese and finish off under the grill.

CONSOMMÉ CUPS [S]

Try these unusual and delicious mushrooms for a dinner party starter. They will convince your guests you are an expert in the Cuisine Nouvelle!

8 large mushrooms, stalks removed
½ pint/300 ml consommé, hot
½ oz/15 g gelatine
4 oz/100 g rich cream cheese
8 walnut halves

Poach the mushrooms in the hot consommé. Drain, put on a dish and chill.

Dissolve the gelatine in 2 tablespoons of the consommé and stir into the remainder of the soup. When cool, place in the fridge to set.

Chop set consommé and use to fill each mushroom, then pipe with a rosette of chilled cream cheese. Top with a walnut and serve chilled.

SPECIAL TIP. To make a mushroom duxelle for lining meat en croûte recipes such as Boeuf Wellington and Lamb Cutlets en Croûte, very finely chop button mushrooms and mix with very finely chopped shallots. Gently fry in butter to soften the vegetables.

MARINATED MUSHROOM AND AVOCADO SALAD   [S]

Choose only really ripe avocados for this salad and mix in at the last minute. Serve on a bed of mixed salad leaves or with Chinese beansprouts.

8 oz/225 g small button mushrooms, quartered
3 fl. oz/75 ml olive oil
1 fl. oz/25 ml fresh lemon juice
1 teaspoon tomato purée
¼ teaspoon dried thyme
pinch fennel seeds
salt and black pepper
3 oz/75 g cashew nuts
¼ green pepper, seeded and finely chopped
2 spring onions, finely chopped
2 teaspoons freshly chopped basil
pinch grated lemon rind
1 large or 2 small avocados, peeled, and stoned and chopped
a few sprigs continental parsley, to garnish

Mix the mushrooms with the olive oil, lemon juice, tomato purée, herbs and seasoning, and leave to stand for at least an hour. Stir from time to time.

Meanwhile dry-fry the cashew nuts in hot frying pan. Keep the nuts on the move or they will burn.

Just before serving add the nuts and all the remaining ingredients to the marinated mushrooms. Toss well together and serve garnished with the parsley.

MUSHROOM AND FENNEL SALAD [S]

The flavours of these two vegetables complement each other particularly well. Serve as a starter on a bed of lettuce or turn it into a main course salad by the addition of 8 oz/225 g cooked and diced chicken meat.

2 small heads or 1 large head Italian fennel, trimmed
6 oz/175 g button mushrooms, quartered or chopped
4 tablespoons thick yogurt, quark low-fat soft cheese, or mayonnaise
a pinch dried thyme or mixed herbs
salt and freshly ground black pepper

Blanch the trimmed heads of fennel in a little boiling salted water for 3—4 minutes or steam for 5—6 minutes in a steamer. Drain, cool and chop.

Mix in with all the other ingredients and serve on a bed of lettuce.

MUSHROOMS IN PARSLEY CREAM SAUCE [S]

This makes a really delicious starter. For a lunch or supper dish, double the quantities and serve with the fried bread cut into triangles and used as a garnish, and new potatoes on the side.

4 thick slices wholemeal bread
4 oz/100 g butter
1 bunch spring onions, finely chopped
8 oz/225 g button mushrooms, sliced
salt and black pepper
¼ pint/150 ml double cream
2 tablespoons freshly chopped parsley

Cut the bread in large rounds with a pastry cutter. Fry in half the butter until crisp and brown on both sides. Drain and keep warm.

Fry the onions and mushrooms in the remaining butter until just softened. Season and pour on the cream. Bring to the boil over a low heat and continue cooking for 3—4 minutes until the sauce thickens. Stir in the parsley, heat through and serve on the rounds of fried bread.

FRENCH MUSHROOM FLANS [A]

These little French flans are turned out and served as an accompaniment to the main dish. However, they could also be served as a starter with a cream sauce or, cooked in a larger mould, as a lunch or supper dish.

1 dessertspoon cooking oil
knob of butter
6 shallots, very finely chopped
4 oz/100 g button mushrooms, very finely chopped
4 oz/100 g raw chicken or turkey meat
milk
1 slice bread, crusts removed
¼ pint/150 ml double cream
salt and pepper

Heat the oil and butter in a pan and fry the shallots for 2—3 minutes. Next add the mushrooms and continue frying over a low heat until the mixture is cooked. Continue frying over a slightly higher heat until the mixture is really dry. This will take about 10 minutes. Stir from time to time. Take care not to burn the mixture. Leave to cool.

Mince the chicken or turkey meat in a food processor. Pour the milk over the bread. Leave for a minute and squeeze out all the liquid. Add the bread to the poultry meat. Continue processing and pour in the cream. Process very quickly and remove from the processor and mix in the seasonings with a fork.

Add the cooled mushroom mixture, mix together, and spoon into 4—6 small greased moulds (use ramekins or dariole moulds). Place in a baking tin filled with 1—2 inches (2.5—5 cm) of very hot water and bake at 190°C/375°F/Gas 5 for about 30 minutes until the flans are well set. Turn one out and test the base to see that they are fully cooked. Turn them all out to serve.

NB: Do not over-process once the cream has been added to the chicken, or the mixture will curdle. It can still be used but the end result will not be quite so smooth.

AVOCADOS

We tend to think of avocados as a relatively new item in UK super-markets, but in fact they were known as long ago as 1692 when an English physician declared that the avocado was 'one of the most rare and pleasant fruits'. And indeed it *is* a fruit though, like tomatoes, we tend to use it more as a vegetable.

Like tomatoes, avocados originated in the New World. They came originally from Central America, and as the Indians moved across the area they took the avocado with them, the Incas introducing the fruit to Peru and the Aztecs to Mexico. Early Spanish records do not mention avocados but they must almost certainly have brought the fruit to Europe. The name pear is something of a misnomer for though the fruit is pear-shaped it bears no relation to our own pear.

Early sailors nicknamed the plant the Butter Pear or Midshipman's Butter for it was eaten on board ship on return sailings from the New World. It is also known as the Alligator Pear, and this probably refers to the texture of the skin of the Hass avocado.

Avocados are rich in oil, which is not so good for slimmers' figures but *is* good for their complexions, and some beauty experts recommend facial masks based on avocado.

Availability: All the year round.

Buying Guide: Most avocados are imported while they are still unripe so test for ripeness by pressing the sharp end with your thumb. However, unripe avocados will ripen at home within a few days of purchase. When buying the soft-skinned green avocados, avoid those with dark patches on the skin as they may be over-ripe. On the other hand a dark colour on the hard-skinned Hass avocados indicates that they are ready to eat.

Storage: Store unripe avocados at room temperature and ripe ones in the fridge where they will keep for a day or so.

Preparation: Do not prepare avocados until they are required as the flesh discolours quickly on contact with air. This can be re-tarded by dipping the cut surfaces of the avocado in lemon juice. Lemon juice will also be needed in any made dishes using avocados such as mousses.

To use, cut the avocado in half lengthways and remove the stone. The centre cavity may be filled with vinaigrette or other sauces. Sometimes the flesh is scooped out and mixed with other ingredients and piled back into the skins. Alternatively, slice the peeled avocados lengthways or horizonally and use to make attractive patterns on the serving plate.

Basic Cooking: Avocados are not often used in cooking but they can be peeled, sliced and baked in lemon juice and butter, scattered with breadcrumbs. Avocado purée also makes an unusual flavouring for sauces, soups and dressings.

SPECIAL TIP. To make an avocado sauce to go with cold meats and salads, mix avocado purée with an equal quantity of mayonnaise and a dash of lemon juice and season to taste.

GUACAMOLE   [S]

This Mexican dip can be made just as mild or spicy as you like. The really authentic version uses crushed dried red peppers, but these can be fiery, and it is easier to check the Tabasco level.

1 avocado, peeled, stone removed
juice of 1 lemon
salt
4 oz/100 g grated onion
a few drops Tabasco sauce
1 teaspoon Worcestershire sauce

Sieve or purée the avocado flesh with the lemon juice. Stir in all the remaining ingredients and chill for 30 minutes.
   Stir again and serve with sliced raw vegetables as dippers. Taco corn chips also make good dippers.

CALIFORNIAN COURGETTE AND AVOCADO SALAD[S]

Courgettes are now grown in California and a friend from Santa Barbara sent this recipe to me.

12 oz/350 g courgettes, sliced
2 oz/50 g cream cheese, cut into small pieces
2 tablespoons salad or olive oil
2 teaspoons cider vinegar
1 teaspoon soy sauce
5—6 spring onions, finely chopped

1 green chilli, seeded and finely chopped
salt and black pepper
1 large ripe avocado
5—6 lettuce leaves

Steam the courgettes in a steamer or in a very little boiling water
for about 3 minutes. Drain well and toss with the cream cheese.

Mix the oil, vinegar, soy sauce, spring onion, chilli and seasonings
in a bowl. Peel and stone the avocado and dice. Mix with the oil
and vinegar mixture and add to the courgettes.

Toss all the ingredients carefully together. Chill for an hour.
Serve on a bed of lettuce with chunks of wholemeal bread.

AVOCADO AND BACON SALAD   [S]

*Avocados lend themselves well to salads. Try them tossed into
green side salads or mixed with lettuce, tomato and cucumber.
This is rather more elaborate, and it makes and excellent starter.*

juice of 2 lemons
a little grated lemon rind
2 tablespoons salad oil
salt and black pepper
2 small to medium avocados, peeled, stoned and diced
4 oz/100 g lean smoked bacon rashers, crisply grilled
2 oz/50 g mushrooms, sliced
2 in/5 cm cucumber, diced
4—5 lettuce leaves

Mix the lemon juice, lemon rind, salad oil, salt and black pepper
in a bowl, and drop in the diced avocado as it is prepared. Add all
the remaining ingredients except the lettuce and toss well together.

Use the lettuce leaves to line a serving dish or shred and use on
four individual plates. Pile the salad on top.

AVOCADO AND CHICORY SALAD   [S]

*This, too, makes an excellent starter, and it is particularly colourful
with the green of the avocado, the red of the radicchio and the
white of the chicory and cheese.*

1 head radicchio, washed
1 large avocado
2 tablespoons lemon juice
3 heads chicory, sliced
2 oz/50 g Edam cheese, diced
8 walnut halves, chopped
2 tablespoons freshly chopped parsley
2 tablespoons plain yogurt
pinch dried thyme

Drain the radicchio well and arrange the separated leaves on four small serving plates.

Peel, stone and dice the avocado into the lemon juice. Add all the remaining ingredients and toss well together. Spoon onto the radicchio and serve with slices of brown bread and butter.

AVOCADO AND ORANGE SALAD   [S]

Avocado mixes well with all citrus fruit. Here's a recipe using oranges but you could just as easily use grapefruit. Make just before serving or the avocados will discolour.

2 large oranges, peeled and sliced into rounds
2 large avocados, peeled, stoned and sliced into lengths
4 tablespoons quark low-fat soft cheese
1 tablespoon cashew nuts, chopped
1 tablespoon raisins

Arrange the orange rounds on four individual plates and arrange two or three slices of avocado between each slice.

Mix the remaining ingredients together and place a spoonful in the centre of each plate. Serve at once.

MARCH

'A bushel of March dust is worth a king's ransom.'

Sixteenth-century proverb

Jerusalem Artichokes
Spinach and Chard
Tomatoes
Garlic

JERUSALEM ARTICHOKES

Jerusalem artichokes are not really artichokes at all. They are actually the tubers of a species of sunflower which were first cultivated in Canada and in the upper valleys of the Mississippi. They take their second name from the fact that their flavour does, indeed, closely resemble that of globe artichokes, but the derivation of the first part of the name is open to speculation. One explanation regards Jerusalem as an anglicisation of 'Ter Neusen', the place in Holland from which the vegetable found its way to Britain. Another says that it is a corruption of 'girasole', Italian for sunflower.

Availability: October to April. They are said to be at their tastiest towards the end of their season.

Buying Guide: All Jerusalem artichokes tend to be rather ugly and knobbly but if you can find a variety called Fuseau there will be fewer of these lumps and they will be easier to peel. Choose similar sized vegetables for uniform cooking if possible.

Storage: Keep in a cool, dark, airy place for up to a week.

Preparation: Scrub very well and thinly peel or cook and peel afterwards. Slice and serve raw with lemon juice — they taste very like water chestnuts.

Basic Cooking: Steam or boil in a very little salted water for 20—30 minutes. Add a little lemon juice to the water for peeled vegetables and take care not to overcook or they will start to split. Serve with butter or white sauce. Alternatively, par-boil and deep-fry in batter or braise in the oven. Jerusalem artichokes can also be cooked whole in a covered casserole with a little stock or in foil. Use in soups and casseroles.

JERUSALEM ARTICHOKE SOUP   [S]

Try this interesting Dutch soup with garlic croûtons. The recipe came from some friends in The Hague who insist that the garlic helps bring out the flavour of the artichokes.

1 small onion, chopped
1 tablespoon cooking oil
12 oz/350 g Jerusalem artichokes
2 carrots, peeled and chopped
2 tomatoes, chopped
1 pint/600 ml chicken stock
salt and black pepper

Fry the onion gently in the cooking oil. Meanwhile wash and peel the artichokes. Wash again, chop and add to the pan.

Add all the remaining ingredients, then bring to the boil, cover and simmer for 45 minutes. Sieve or purée in a blender. Reheat and serve.

ARTICHOKES JERUSALEM   [A]

This recipe uses Jerusalem artichokes in a manner which might well be found in the city of their name.

1 large onion, chopped
2 tablespoons olive oil
1½lb/700 g large Jerusalem artichokes
4 tomatoes, peeled and chopped
1 tablespoon tomato purée
½ teaspoon dried dill
salt and black pepper
juice of 1 lemon
2 tablespoons chopped parsley
¼ pint/150 ml water

Fry the onion in hot olive oil until well browned. Meanwhile wash and peel the artichokes and wash again. Cut into quarters and add to the onion. Toss well so that they are coated in oil.

Add all the remaining ingredients, stir and bring to the boil. Cover and simmer, stirring from time to time, for 30—35 minutes, until the Jerusalem artichokes are just tender and the sauce is thick.

CREAMY ARTICHOKE CASSEROLE   [A]

This unusual treatment of Jerusalem artichokes goes particularly well with baked ham.

1½ lb/700 g Jerusalem artichokes, well scrubbed
2 onions, peeled
3 tablespoons cream or soft cheese
salt and pepper
4 tablespoons wholemeal breadcrumbs

Steam the artichokes and the whole onions in a steamer for about 35–40 minutes until the artichokes are soft, or boil in a little water for about 20–25 minutes. Drain and peel the artichokes.

Mash the onions and peeled artichokes together. Stir in the cream cheese and seasonings. Spoon into a heatproof casserole or pie dish. Sprinkle with breadcrumbs and bake at 190°C/375°F/ Gas 5 for 30 minutes.

SPINACH AND CHARD

Spinach was a relative latecomer to British shores. The Dutch introduced it to European cookery, and it came originally from Asia. In Elizabethan times, chefs liked to use a purée of spinach in sweet tarts. Today it is strictly a savoury dish, but the cooking advice 'fry in its own juice', given in an early cookbook, still holds good. The resultant pulp may be tossed in butter with herbs and spices, or puréed and used as the base for dishes cooked in the 'Florentine' manner, or in soufflés, mousses and salads.

The leaves of Swiss chard have a similar taste to spinach but the stalks are much thicker and wider and can be cooked with the leaves or separately.

Availability: Spinach all the year round; Swiss chard in the late autumn and the spring.

Buying Guide: Both spinach and Swiss chard should be clean and bright in colour. Avoid any with very limp or yellowing leaves. Spinach shrinks substantially on cooking so allow at least 8 oz/ 225 g per person. Chard does not shrink quite so much since the stalks add bulk.

Storage: Use as soon as possible after purchase. However, it can be washed and stored in a polythene box in the fridge for a day or so.

Preparation: Wash spinach and use the leaves whole in salads or in cooking. Wash Swiss chard and cook the leaves whole. Cut the stalks into slices.

Basic Cooking: Place washed spinach in the pan and cook over a gentle heat. Do not add any water at all. When cooked drain very well and serve chopped with butter. Cook Swiss chard with a little water and treat as spinach. The stalks may be cut off and sautéed in butter as a separate dish.

SPINACH GNOCCHI [S]

A good deal of Italian pasta is flavoured with spinach. This recipe uses spinach to flavour a light semolina-based gnocchi. Serve as a starter with tomato sauce (see page 46).

1½ lb/700 g spinach, picked over and stalks removed
14 fl. oz/400 ml milk
2 oz/50 g semolina
1 small egg (size 6), beaten
2 oz/50 g Parmesan cheese, grated
¼ teaspoon grated nutmeg
salt and pepper

Wash the spinach, shake dry and cook without any water for about 5—8 minutes. Drain and chop the spinach and dry over a low heat. Stir in the milk and then the semolina. Bring to the boil, stirring all the time. Continue stirring and cooking over a low heat until the mixture is really stiff.

Remove from the heat and beat in the egg, cheese and seasonings. Leave to cool and chill in the fridge for 2 hours.

Shape the mixture into large almonds with dessertspoons and drop into gently simmering water. Cook for about 5 minutes until all the gnocchi have risen to the surface. Serve at once.

GRATIN OF PRAWNS WITH CHARD [S]

I first had this dish at a beautiful restaurant perched high over the Mediterranean near Monte Carlo. It makes an excellent starter, or it can be served as a main course. In the latter case, double the quantities.

12 large cooked prawns in their shells
¼ pint/150 ml white wine
12 leaves Swiss chard
1 oz/25 g butter
grated nutmeg
7 fl. oz/200 ml double cream
3 egg yolks
black pepper

Peel the prawns, slice and keep on one side. Retain the shells and place in a pan with the white wine. Bring to the boil and simmer for 30 minutes. Strain and reduce the liquid by boiling to about 2 fl. oz/50 ml.

Wash the chard and separate the stems from the leaves. Steam in a steamer or a very little water until tender. Drain well. Slice the stems, fry in a little butter to brown them, and sprinkle with nutmeg.

Place a little of the fried chard stems in the centre of four shallow heatproof gratin dishes and arrange the leaves round the sides. Sprinkle with a little grated nutmeg. Place the shelled prawns on top and heat through in a low oven.

Meanwhile lightly whisk the cream and stir in the egg yolks. Pour into the strained prawn liquid and whisk over a low heat with a wire whisk. Add the black pepper and continue whisking until the sauce thickens. Do not allow the sauce to boil. Remove from the heat and pour over the prawns. Place under a hot grill until a thin golden skin forms on the surface. Serve immediately.

SPINACH GRATIN   [A]

This is a classic French dish which I learned how to prepare on a cookery course in Deauville.

2 lb/1 kg spinach, washed and picked over
1 tablespoon raisins
¼ teaspoon grated nutmeg
¼ pint/150 ml double cream

Drain the spinach and place in a saucepan over a medium to low heat. Cover and bring to the boil in the liquid which comes off the leaves. Cook for about 5 minutes until the leaves have just softened.

Drain well and place in layers in a shallow earthenware dish sprinkling with raisins as you go. Sprinkle with nutmeg and pour on the cream. Bake at 200°C/400°F/Gas 6 for about 20 minutes.

SPINACH CROUSTADE [A]

This French tart makes a pleasant change from the ubiquitous quiche. Serve for lunch or supper or as part of an informal hot buffet..

1 onion, finely chopped
1 clove garlic, chopped
½ oz/15 g butter
10 oz/300 g lean beef, minced
6 oz/175 g veal or pork, minced
1 tablespoon tomato purée
1 dessertspoon flour
4 tablespoons dry white wine
2 tablespoons Parmesan cheese, grated
salt and freshly ground black pepper
1 lb/450 g frozen chopped spinach
grated nutmeg
8 oz/225 g shortcrust pastry

Fry the onion and garlic in butter for a minute or two and then add the meats. Cook for a further 5 minutes, stirring from time to time. Add the tomato purée, flour and white wine. Stir well and continue cooking over a gentle heat for about 10 minutes. Stir in half the cheese and a little seasoning and leave to cool.

Meanwhile place the spinach in a saucepan and thaw over a gentle heat. Turn up the heat and dry off all the moisture. Season and add a little grated nutmeg. Leave to cool.

Roll out the pastry and use to line an 8 in/20 cm flan tin. Spoon half the meat mixture into the base of the flan. Cover with the spinach. Spoon the rest of the meat mixture over the top. Sprinkle with the remaining Parmesan, and bake at 200°C/400°F/ Gas 6 for 50–60 minutes. Serve hot.

TOMATOES

Originating in South America, the first tomatoes to be cultivated in the UK were grown mainly as a garden ornament and were known as 'love apples'. They were yellow in colour and were probably about the size of cherry tomatoes. Because it was a member of the nightshade family, early botanists thought that the tomato was poisonous, and it was said that only a hapless lover or a potential suicide would toy with a tomato!

The Italians were the first to cultivate the fruit for this is what it is. It was called 'pomodoro' and has given its name to special sauces for pasta and other dishes. Both the Italian and Spanish cuisines use tomatoes extensively in soups, sauces, casseroles, salads and rice dishes, and often combine it with other vegetables such as peppers and aubergines. In France the Provençal cuisine also uses a good many tomatoes, often in conjunction with garlic or basil.

Availability: All the year round with home-grown tomatoes available from March to November.

Buying Guide: At their best, tomatoes should be hard, sweet and juicy with a good shape and colour. These will be classed as Extra or Class I. Classes II and III may be more irregular in shape but should be free of open cracks. Fresh samples have a faint aromatic smell, and the calyx on top of the fruit will not be withered. Beef or Continental tomatoes are larger than the usual English varieties and can have more flavour.

Storage: Store ripe samples in a cool place for two to three days. Unripe tomatoes may be ripened in a paper bag in a drawer by placing one ripe one with the others.

Preparation: Wash tomatoes and serve raw or cooked, whole, halved or sliced. To peel, drop into boiling water for a few seconds or hold over a gas flame, turning the tomato so that all the skin is exposed to the heat, then rub off the skin. To remove seeds, quarter and scoop out with a teaspoon.

Basic Cooking: Fry or grill whole or halved tomatoes. Bake tomatoes stuffed or topped with breadcrumbs and herbs. Halve and fill with cooked peas or sweetcorn. Purée and use in hot and cold sauces, dressings and soups. Chop or slice and use in salads and casseroles.

CHILLED TOMATO SOUP WITH FRESH BASIL [S]

There is nothing quite like a really good fresh tomato soup. This soup can be served hot but it is better chilled.

1 small carrot, finely chopped
1 leek, finely chopped
1 shallot, finely chopped
1 clove garlic (optional), finely chopped
1½ tablespoons olive oil
1½ pints/900 ml chicken stock
1 sprig fresh thyme or a pinch dried
1 bay leaf
salt and pepper
1½ lb/700 g ripe tomatoes, peeled and seeded
1 tablespoon tomato purée
1 tablespoon freshly chopped basil
1 dessertspoon sugar

Gently fry the carrot, leek, shallot and garlic (if used) in 1 table-spoon of the olive oil. Cook for 4—5 minutes and then add the stock, herbs and seasoning. Add the tomato flesh and tomato purée and bring to the boil. Simmer, uncovered for 20 minutes.

Sieve or purée in a blender and leave to cool. Chill in the fridge. Just before serving mix the remaining oil, the basil and sugar, and stir into the soup.

PROVENCE TOMATOES [S]

Serve with plenty of crusty bread to mop up the filling. In France the choice would be a thin baguette, but any kind of French bread will do.

8 medium-sized tomatoes
1—2 cloves garlic to taste, crushed
8 tablespoons freshly chopped parsley
¼ pint/150 ml olive oil
freshly ground black pepper
sprigs of parsley to garnish

Cut a slice off the tops of the tomatoes and keep on one side. Scoop out the centres and the pulp, discarding the hard centres. Mix the pulp with the garlic, parsley, olive oil and pepper.

Spoon back into the empty tomatoes and close up with the retained tomato tops. Chill for at least an hour before serving. Garnish with a small sprig of parsley on top of each tomato.

FRIED TOMATOES WITH SOURED CREAM SAUCE　　　[S]

This idea comes from central Europe where soured cream is a popular base for sauces. The large Continental tomatoes are the best type to use for this recipe. But large English tomatoes could be used instead.

4 Continental tomatoes, peeled and thickly sliced
salt and pepper
2 eggs, beaten
4 slices stale wholemeal bread, made into breadcrumbs
1 oz/25 g butter
2 tablespoons oil
3 fl. oz/75 ml soured cream
1 tablespoon freshly chopped chives

Dry the slices of tomato on kitchen paper. Season and dip first in beaten egg and then in breadcrumbs. Make sure that the tomatoes are fully coated.

Heat the butter and oil in a frying pan and fry the tomato slices on both sides until crisp and golden. If necessary fry in batches and keep warm. Mix the soured cream and chives together and serve with the fried tomatoes.

EGG AND TARRAGON TOMATOES　　　[S]

The three flavours of egg, tarragon and tomato complement each other well. Here I have used them to make an easy starter.

12 medium or 8 large tomatoes
4 eggs, beaten
4 tablespoons quark low-fat soft cheese
1 teaspoon dried tarragon
salt and pepper

Slice the tops off the tomatoes. Scoop out the pulp and discard. Place on a lightly greased ovenproof plate. Mix the eggs with the soft cheese and beat well to remove any lumps. Add the tarragon and seasoning and spoon the mixture into the hollowed-out tomatoes. Bake at 190°C/375°F/Gas 5 for 30 minutes.

EGG AND SAVORY TOMATOES [S]

As a variation on the above, substitute 4 oz/100g puréed cooked peas for 3 tablespoons of the quark and add 1 tablespoon of savory instead of the tarragon, and continue as above.

STUFFED TOMATOES [S]

A quick and simple tomato recipe. The flavour can be varied with the use of different pâté spreads.

8 tomatoes
4 oz/100 g ham and tongue pâté spread
4 oz/100 g garlic sausage, diced
2 oz/50 g fresh breadcrumbs
1 dessert apple, peeled, cored and chopped
1 teaspoon oregano
1 tablespoon chopped parsley
salt and pepper

Cut the tops of the tomatoes and put on one side. Carefully scoop out the flesh and chop. Miz the remaining ingredients together and spoon back into the tomato shells.

Place the filled tomatoes in a lightly greased ovenproof dish and replace the lids. Bake in a preheated oven at 180°C/350°F/Gas 4 for 20—25 minutes.

TOMATO AND YOGURT SALAD WITH FRESH HERBS [A]

This simple but delicious salad goes well with grilled meats. I also like it as a light starter to a heavier meal.

1 lb/450 g English or Continental tomatoes
3 tablespoons natural yogurt
1 tablespoon freshly chopped parsley, mint, thyme, basil or
    rosemary
salt and black pepper

Quickly immerse the tomatoes in boiling water, and then peel them. Slice and arrange on individual serving plates.

Mix the yogurt with your chosen herb and the seasoning. Pour over the tomatoes and serve.

FRESH TOMATO SAUCE [A]

Depending on the foods with which you plan to serve this simple sauce, flavour with ¼ teaspoon dried rosemary, basil or tarragon or a pinch of fennel seeds or dried thyme.

2 lb/1 kg ripe tomatoes, chopped
1 tablespoon tomato purée
salt and pepper

Place all the ingredients in a saucepan and bring slowly to the boil. Reduce the heat and simmer for 30 minutes. Rub through a sieve.

GARLIC

Garlic was first grown in Central Asia, but it has been cultivated in the Mediterranean area since early Egyptian times. The slaves who built the Pyramids were said by Pliny to have subsisted mainly on a diet of garlic and onions, and he maintained that garlic was an energy food. Others write of athletes eating garlic for physical fitness, and folk medicine has always regarded it as a guard against all kinds of ills ranging from colds to witchcraft!

Garlic is usually thought of as a flavouring rather than a vegetable in its own right. However, in France, large fresh heads of garlic are roasted whole and eaten with butter and jacket potatoes, or whole cloves are roasted with the joint. Garlic cooked in this way loses a good deal of its pungency. Parsley, particularly the stalks, can be used to counteract the strong garlic flavours, produced by crushing or chopping cloves of garlic, and chewing the stalks is thought to reduce the smell of garlic on the breath.

Availability: Fresh during the summer and dried all the year round.

Buying Guide: Check dried garlic to see that the head is not to old and the cloves completely dried up.

Storage: Keep in a cool, airy, dark place.

Preparation: Use whole as suggested above or, more usually, break into cloves. Use to cook or rub round salad bowls. Peel and chop or crush.

Basic Cooking: Mix with butter and herbs for garlic bread or as a sauce for snails, mussels and mushrooms. Use to flavour casseroles and sauces.

GARLIC BREAD [A]

This is a favourite with almost everyone. Add the stalks as well as the leaves of the finely chopped parsley and you will have more chance of being reasonably socially acceptable the day after eating it!

3—4 cloves garlic, crushed
3 tablespoons freshly chopped parsley
pinch dried thyme
black pepper
4 oz/100 g softened butter
a little grated lemon rind
1 long French loaf

Place all the ingredients — apart from the loaf — in a bowl and blend well together. Cut the loaf into slices and cover each slice generously with the garlic butter mixture. Push the slices together to reform the loaf and wrap in foil.

Bake at 210°C/425°F/Gas 7 for about 5—10 minutes until warm and crisp. Serve from the foil.

NB: Garlic butter can be delicious on grilled steak or stuffed under the skin of a chicken before roasting.

PESTO SAUCE FOR PASTA [A]

It is essential to use fresh basil in this classic recipe for the Italian pasta sauce which comes from Liguria on the Italian Riviera.

2 oz/50 g fresh basil leaves
2 cloves garlic
2 tablespoons pine kernels
pinch salt
1 oz/25 g Parmesan cheese, finely grated
50—75 ml/2—3 fl. oz olive oil

Very finely chop the basil leaves, garlic and pine kernels or grind together in a mortar. Add the salt and cheese and then stir in the oil a little at a time. If possible finish off in a blender.

Pour over freshly cooked and drained pasta.

AÏOLI   [A]

Aioli is a garlic-packed sauce traditionally served with steamed or poached fish, but it can also be served with cold meat or cooked vegetable salads, or as a dip with crudité. Adjust the quantities of garlic to taste.

4—6 cloves garlic, peeled
1 egg yolk
salt
scant ½ pint/250 ml olive oil

In a large bowl, mash and pound the garlic to a fine pulp and mix with the egg yolk. Season with salt and gradually mix in the olive oil, adding a little at a time as for mayonnaise. Continue stirring vigorously and mixing in the oil until the sauce has thickened and most of the oil is used up.

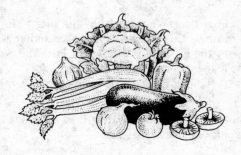

APRIL

'Happy is said to be the family which can eat onions together. They are, for the time being, separate from the world, and have a harmony of aspiration.'

Charles Dudley Warner (1871)

Radishes
Turnips
Watercress
Spring Onions

RADISHES

Radishes are among the oldest known vegetables, and probably originated in China where they were cultivated in the seventh century BC. They were popular in Ancient Egypt and also in Greece and Rome. Cowper refers to a Roman meal as 'a radish and an egg', and in ancient Rome both were used to pelt unpopular politicians.

In Medieval Britain radishes were well known, and at one time they were grown in every garden because they grew so fast and easily. These radishes were probably the pinkish red salad radishes that we know today. But this peppery root can come in all colours and shapes and sizes. In Spain the radishes are large and black and full of flavour. Salad radishes are usually eaten raw, and in France and in the Far East they are eaten with butter.

Horseradish is much stronger in flavour, dark in colour and longer than salad radishes. Other 'hot' radishes are the white mouli or Japanese horseradish.

Availability: Salad radishes are available almost all the year round. Home-grown radishes last from March until October.

Buying Guide: Choose salad radishes which are bright in colour and, if not pre-packed, have fresh green leaves. Horseradishes should be firm and straight.

Storage: Keep salad radishes for one or two days in the salad compartment of the fridge.

Preparation: Top and tail salad radishes and wash. Eat raw. To make radish 'flowers' make four or five cuts lengthways in the radish or cut 'petals' all round the outside and soak in water. The 'flowers' will open up in the water. Peel and grate horseradish for use in made dishes and horseradish sauce.

RADISHES IN YOGURT SAUCE   [S]

Radishes are not often cooked, though in France they are sometimes steamed and served hot with butter. This recipe comes from Bulgaria and any mild variety of radish may be used.

2 bunches radishes, topped, tailed and washed
5 oz/150 g natural yogurt
2 egg yolks
1 teaspoon lemon juice
½ teaspoon made mustard
salt and pepper
2 tablespoons freshly chopped parsley
3—4 gherkins, very finely chopped

Steam the radishes in a steamer or in a very little boiling water for 5—8 minutes. Drain well.

Beat the yogurt, egg yolks and lemon juice together in a bowl and place over a pan of simmering water. Whisk over the heat with a wire whisk until the sauce begins to thicken. This takes about 10—15 minutes. Season with mustard, salt and pepper and leave to cool a little.

Arrange the radishes on a plate. Stir the parsley and gherkins into the sauce and spoon over the radishes. Serve lukewarm or leave to cool completely.

RADISH AND CARROT SALAD [A]

Long white carrot-shaped radishes are now available in many supermarkets and in continental shops.

1 small long white radish, peeled
8 oz/225 g carrots, peeled

Dressing
4 tablespoons wine vinegar
1 tablespoon soy sauce
1 teaspoon sugar

Cut the radish and the carrots into thin 1 in/2.5 cm sticks. Plunge into boiling water for 3 minutes and then drain and plunge into cold water to refresh. Drain again and put into a serving bowl.

Mix the dressing ingredients together and pour over the salad. Toss and serve.

HORSERADISH SAUCE FOR STEAK [A]

I have adapted the traditional combination of horseradish sauce with roast beef to make a really delicious sauce for steak.

3 shallots or 1 very small onion, very finely chopped
1 oz/25 g butter
1 oz/25 grated horseradish
1 tablespoon cider or wine vinegar
2 tablespoons freshly chopped parsley
salt and freshly ground black pepper
¼ pint/150 ml double cream
2 tablespoons milk

Fry the shallots or onion in butter until lightly browned. Add the horseradish, vinegar, parsley and seasoning. Cook very gently for 10 minutes, stirring from time to time.

Pour on the cream and milk and bring to the boil. Cook for 1—2 minutes until thoroughly heated through. Pour over the cooked steak and serve.

TURNIPS

There is some confusion over the name turnips, for in Northern England and in Scotland the term 'neeps' is sometimes used for swede. However, turnips here mean the small white vegetables which may be available in bunches or loose.

No one knows where turnips originated, but it is likely to have been the Middle East. They were known to the Sumerians, one of the earliest civilisations, and both the Greeks and Romans grew them. It is probable that the Romans introduced turnips to Britain. Improved varieties were cultivated by Flemish immigrants in Elizabethan times and they have been around every since. In Roman and Elizabethan times, turnips were served with roast duck, and they can easily be par-boiled and then roasted in the oven with the duck.

Both turnips and turnip tops are good to eat and they are good sources of Vitamin C, dietary fibre and minerals.

Availability: Bunched April to July, and maincrop from August to March.

Buying Guide: Choose bunched turnips with fresh green leaves, and maincrop turnips which are firm and free from worm holes.

Storage: Eat bunched turnips as soon as possible and store main-crop in a cool, dry, airy place away from light.

Preparation: Very young turnips can be scrubbed and used whole or quartered, but older ones will need to be thinly peeled. Cut out any green patches and grate for salads or slice, cube or dice for cooking. Young turnip tops can be washed and shredded for cooking.

Basic Cooking: Steam or boil in a very little salted water until just tender. Serve tossed in butter or cream and flavour with fresh herbs. Turnips may also be served cooked, diced or grated and chilled in salads with apples and nuts or a sour cream and lemon dressing, or they can be used to flavour casseroles and soups. Turnips go particularly well with duck and with ham.

TURNIPS WITH LAMB   [M]

This Middle Eastern recipe makes an unusual winter warmer, and is good with either rice or potatoes.

1½ lb/700 g lean lamb, cut into pieces
½ teaspoon turmeric
½ teaspoon dried oregano
salt and black pepper
juice of 1 lemon
1 tablespoon tomato purée
1 lb/450 g turnips, prepared and diced

Place all the ingredients except the turnips in a saucepan and barely cover with water. Bring to the boil, cover and simmer for 45 minutes. Add the turnips and continue cooking for a further 30 minutes until the meat and turnips are both very tender.

TURNIPS AU GRATIN   [M]

This makes a good supper dish or it can be served with a plain roast duck.

1 lb/450 g turnips, prepared and sliced
3 oz/75 g butter
2 oz/50 g flour
½ pint/300 ml milk

2 oz/50 g strong Gruyère or Cheddar cheese, grated
grated nutmeg
½ oz/15 breadcrumbs
½ oz/15 g Parmesan cheese, grated

Gently fry the turnip slices in 1 oz/25 g of the butter until tender.

Meanwhile make the sauce. Melt the remaining butter in a pan, add the flour and milk, and bring quickly to the boil, whisking with a wire whisk. Simmer gently for 3 minutes, stirring constantly, until the sauce is thick. Add grated Gruyère or Cheddar cheese and the nutmeg.

Layer the cheese sauce in a pie dish or casserole with the turnips, finishing with a layer of cheese sauce. Sprinkle the breadcrumbs and Parmesan evenly on the surface and place under the grill until golden brown.

FRICASSÉE OF TURNIP WITH HAM   [A]

This was inspired by an Elizabethan recipe. Serve with roast chicken and a green vegetable.

1 onion, finely chopped
½ oz/15 g butter
1 lb/450 g small young turnips, quartered
½ oz/15 g flour
½ pint/300 ml chicken stock
4 oz/100 g ham, diced
pinch dried thyme
pinch sugar
salt and pepper

Fry the onion in the butter until golden brown in a saucepan. Add the turnips and heat and cook for a few moments. Stir in the flour, cook for a minute and then add the chicken stock. Bring to the boil, stirring all the time.

Add ham, thyme, sugar and seasonings and simmer, covered, for 40 minutes.

WATERCRESS

This aquatic plant was well known to the Greeks who believed it would cure a deranged mind. Indeed there is a Greek proverb which says 'Eat cress and get more wit', and some people still believe that munching fresh watercress when drinking alcohol keeps you sober. Folk medicine also maintains that watercress is good for rheumatism and for easing headaches and warding off migraine. Be that as it may, it makes an excellent salad vegetable and can be used as a flavouring in flans and soups.

Watercress is certainly very good for health. It contains plenty of Vitamin C, even more Vitamin A, and ten times more calcium than any other vegetable, as well as Vitamin B, iron and dietary fibre. To get the most out of the iron content eat raw with fruit, such as oranges, which are high in Vitamin C.

Availability: All the year round, but supplies tend to dwindle in very cold weather. It is at its peak during the period March to May.

Buying Guide: Choose watercress with dark green glossy leaves and avoid any with yellow leaves or wilting stems.

Storage: Wash and drain and keep in a container in the salad drawer of the fridge for two to three days, or stand stems in a jug of water and keep in a cool place.

Preparation: Wash well and cut off the stalks when using for salads. Use up the stalks in soups and stews.

Basic Cooking: Cook with no water over a gentle heat. Drain well and chop for use in omelettes, quiches and sauces. Use also in hot and cold soups and in cold stuffings and dressings.

WATERCRESS CANNELLONI   [S]

Plainly minced chicken or spinach and cottage cheese are more usual fillings for cannelloni, but watercress really adds an extra dimension to the dish. Serve with a home-made tomato sauce (see page 46).

8 cannelloni shells
salt
1 bunch watercress, very finely chopped
6 oz/175 g cooked chicken meat, minced

7 oz/200 g quark low-fat soft cheese
¾ oz/20 g butter
¾ oz/20 g flour
¾ pint/450 ml milk
2 tablespoons grated Parmesan cheese
freshly ground black pepper

Cook the cannelloni shells in plenty of salted boiling water as directed on the pack. Mix the watercress, chicken and cheese and use to stuff the cooked and drained cannelloni. Arrange in the base of four individual heatproof dishes.

Melt the butter in a pan and stir in the flour. Add the milk and bring to the boil, whisking all the time with a wire whisk. Add the cheese and seasonings and cook for 3 minutes. Pour over the cannelloni and bake at 200°C/400°F/Gas 6 for 30 minutes.

HADDOCK AND WATERCRESS MOUSSE   [S]

I serve this pretty green mousse as a starter for six people, or as part of a buffet menu.

2 packets gelatine
juice of 1 lemon
4 oz/100 g open cup mushrooms, wiped clean and sliced
1 bunch watercress
8 oz/225 g smoked haddock
¼ pint/150 ml skimmed milk
1 x 5 oz/150 g carton natural yogurt
1 egg, separated
1 tablespoon horseradish sauce
freshly milled black pepper and salt

Dissolve gelatine in lemon juice in a basin over a pan of hot water. Cool, then make up to 7 fl. oz/200 ml with water. Place spoonfuls of lemon jelly mixture to just cover the base of a 1½ pint/900 ml soufflé dish. Place in refrigerator until set.

Arrange about four-fifths of the thin mushroom slices over the jelly, then place 3 small sprigs of watercress between the mushrooms. Carefully cover with a little more jelly, then return to the refrigerator until set.

Cook haddock in milk for about 8–10 minutes, then remove fish and reserve the strained milk. Remove and discard skin, then place haddock, remaining mushrooms and watercress into a liquidiser or food processor, and blend for about 30 seconds. Turn mixture into a basin, then beat in yoghurt, egg yolk, horseradish sauce, seasoning, reserved milk and remaining lemon jelly. Whisk egg white until stiff, then fold into haddock mixture. Turn into soufflé dish and return to refrigerator until set. To serve, dip dish in hot water for a few seconds, then invert on to plate.

WATERCRESS SOUFFLÉ [M]

Watercress gives a good flavour to this classic soufflé. Serve as a lunch or supper dish, or as a starter for a special meal.

2 bunches watercress
3 oz/75 butter
2 oz/50 g plain flour
½ pint/300 ml milk
2 oz/50 g Cheddar cheese, grated
½ teaspoon dry mustard
salt and black pepper
4 eggs, separated

Blanch the watercress in boiling water for 3 minutes. Drain very well and chop finely. Melt the butter in a pan and stir in the flour. Gradually add the milk, stirring all the time. Bring to the boil and add the cheese, mustard, seasonings and watercress. Cook for 3 minutes.

Remove from the heat and beat in the egg yolks. Whisk the egg whites until stiff. Mix a tablespoon of the white into the sauce, and then fold in the rest. Spoon into a 2 pint/1 litre soufflé dish and bake at 190°C/375°F/Gas 5 for 45 minutes until the soufflé is well risen and firm to the touch in the centre.

COLD WATERCRESS FLAN [M]

This is one of my favourite cold buffet dishes. It's also good to serve on a warm spring evening.

6 oz/175 shortcrust pastry
1 bunch watercress, washed and drained
4 sticks celery, chopped
8 oz/225 g cottage cheese
salt and pepper
2 oz/50 g walnuts, halved

Roll out the pastry and use to line an 8 in/20 cm flan tin. Prick the base all over with a fork and line with foil and dried beans. Bake blind at 200°C/400°F/Gas 6 for about 30 minutes until cooked. Remove the foil and beans after about 15–20 minutes to prevent them sticking to the pastry. Remove from the oven and leave to cool.

Pick out about half a dozen sprigs of watercress from the bunch and coarsely chop the rest. Use the latter to line the cold flan case. Mix the celery with the cottage cheese and season to taste. Spoon into the centre of the flan leaving a little of the watercress showing. Place the walnuts round the edges on top of the watercress and decorate the centre with the sprigs of watercress. Serve at once.

WATERCRESS STUFFING FOR EGGS   [M]

Stuffed eggs make an easy starter, or they can be served in other salads as part of a cold main course. For a stronger flavour, add some grated Cheddar instead of the quark low-fat soft cheese.

6 hard-boiled eggs
1 bunch watercress, well picked over
5–6 tablespoons quark low-fat soft cheese
1½ tablespoons mayonnaise
salt and pepper

Remove the yolks from the eggs and rub through a sieve. Finely chop the watercress, retaining a few sprigs for decoration. Add the chopped watercress to the egg yolks, then add all the remaining ingredients and mix well together.

Spoon back into the whites and garnish with a few sprigs of watercress.

SPRING ONIONS

These are seedling onions which have been dug up before they start to swell too much. They are usually used in salads and dressings, although it's quite easy to use too many. The Reverend Sidney Smith, a noted nineteenth-century gourmet, gave the following advice in his 'Recipe for a Salad':

'Let onion atoms lurk within the bowl,
And scarce suspected, animate the whole,'

Spring onions are sometimes chopped and used in cooked dishes in Continental cooking, though shallots are a more frequent choice. However, the spring onion really comes into its own in Chinese cooking. They are one of the major flavourings along with garlic, ginger and soy sauce.

Availability: All the year round.

Buying Guide: Choose fresh bunches with no sliminess or discoloured tops. Generally speaking the thinner they are the milder they will be.

Storage: Store trimmed and washed in a polythene bag in the salad drawer of the fridge.

Preparation: Trim roots and damaged tops. Remove outer skins if dirty. Slice lengthways, chop or snip with sharp kitchen scissors.

Basic Cooking: Use in stir-fry dishes or in sauces, dressing and stuffings.

GREEN GODDESS DIP [S]

The Americans are very keen on dips as appetisers and this recipe came from a friend in Washington.

8 oz/225 g low-fat soft cheese
2½ tablespoons mayonnaise
1 clove garlic, crushed
green spring onion tips, chopped (6—8 onions, depending on size)
freshly chopped parsley
Worcestershire sauce to taste

Mix all the ingredients together in a bowl. Add a little milk to thin the dip if necessary.

CHOPPED EGG AND ONION   [S]

Use this traditional Jewish favourite for sandwiches and canapés.

4 hard-boiled eggs, finely chopped
10 spring onions, finely chopped
2 tablespoons quark low-fat soft cheese
dash wine vinegar
salt and pepper

Mix all the ingredients together in a bowl and use as required.

BREAST OF CHICKEN WITH SPRING ONIONS AND PAPRIKA
[M]

Good enough for any dinner party! Cut down on the vinegar if the flavour is too strong for your taste.

4 breasts of chicken, boned
flour
salt and pepper
1 tablespoon cooking oil
2 oz/50 g butter
2 bunches spring onions, very finely chopped
1 tablespoon paprika pepper
2 tablespoons wine vinegar
¼ pint/150 ml double cream

Toss the chicken breasts in flour and seasoning and shake off any excess. Heat the cooking oil with ½ oz/15 g of the butter and fry the chicken all over. Continue frying for about 10 minutes on each side until well cooked through. Remove from the pan and keep warm.

Add the remaining butter and the spring onions and fry until they turn transparent. Stir in the paprika and then the vinegar. Bring to the boil and reduce until almost dry. Pour in the cream and bring to the boil. Cook for 5 minutes.

Return the chicken breasts to the pan and cook for a few more minutes until the sauce is fairly thick. Serve at once.

BEEF WITH GINGER AND SPRING ONIONS [M]

This Chinese dish may be made in a large frying pan or, if you have one, in a wok. Keep all the ingredients on the move in the pan and take care not to overcook.

2 in/5 cm piece of root ginger, peeled and cut into sticks
2 bunches spring onions, topped and cut in two
½ clove garlic, crushed (optional)
2 tablespoons cooking oil
2 tablespoons soy sauce
1½ lb/700 g fillet or sirloin steak, cut into thin slivers
1 x 5 oz/150 g can bamboo shoots, drained and cut into sticks
2 tablespoons dry sherry
pinch five-spice powder (optional)

Fry the ginger, spring onions and garlic (if used) in cooking oil for 1 minute. (Split the spring onions lengthways if they are very fat.) Add the soy sauce and the beef and stir-fry for a further minute.

Add the remaining ingredients and continue to stir-fry for 1 minute. Serve with Chinese noodles or rice and Fried Kale with Almonds (see page 9).

MAY

'Let no man boast himself that he has got through the perils of winter till at least the seventh of May.'

Dr Thorne (1858),
Anthony Trollope
(1815—1882)

Asparagus
Peppers
New Potatoes
Mangetout

ASPARAGUS

This expensive vegetable used to grow wild on the shores of the Mediterranean. No one knows how it developed from its wild state to the luxury item it is today. However, it was already well established in the second century BC. The Romans were particularly fond of asparagus with thick white stems, and the growers of Argenteuil agree with them. There the asparagus is grown underground and is completely white.

Here, the tendency is not to blanch the stems by too much banking up, and UK asparagus is thus usually greener in colour than that sold on the Continent.

Never serve asparagus with red wine, for the sulphur in the asparagus will mar the taste of the wine.

Availability: May to June, but the season may extend a little beyond these limits if the weather is good.

Buying Guide: Asparagus is sold graded, with the most expensive having the thickest and whitest stems. Some small thin asparagus is sold as sprue and this can have a very good flavour indeed. The heads should be tight and the stalks fresh looking. Avoid loose bundles and wrinkled dry stalks. If the stalks are wet, however, they may have been standing in water to revive them.

Storage: Eat as soon after purchase as possible. Keep in a cool place until needed.

Preparation: Wash and scrape off any hard, woody parts from the base of the stem. Trim sticks to the same size and tie into bundles with the heads all at one end.

Basic Cooking: Stand the bundles in boiling water, making sure that the heads are not covered for these cook faster than the stems and will fall off. A good way to keep the bundles upright is to place them in the base of a double pan with the inner pan upended over the top. Cook for 11—12 minutes unless very thick. Serve with butter or a butter-based sauce such as hollandaise or mousseline. Serve cold with vinaigrette or use in sauces, soups, flans and mousses.

TARRAGON SAUCE FOR ASPARAGUS [S]

Fresh tarragon goes very well with asparagus. This idea offers an unusual alternative to hot butter or hollandaise sauce.

1 tablespoon freshly chopped tarragon
1 tablespoon freshly chopped parsley
8 fl. oz/225 ml double cream
2 egg yolks
salt and pepper

Retain the cooking liquor from the asparagus and keep the asparagus warm. Boil up the liquid very fast to reduce it to 2 fl. oz/ 50 ml. Add the herbs and leave to cool.

Beat the cream and egg yolks together and pour into the cooled herb liquor. Place over a moderate heat and season to taste. Whisk over the heat with a wire whisk until the sauce thickens.

The sauce is ready when it coats the back of a wooden spoon sufficiently for your finger to leave a mark. Take care not to boil the sauce or it will separate.

PEPPERS

The peppers which Columbus brought back from the New World were originally called 'Calcutta Peppers' because it was thought that Columbus had reached India.

There are two types of capsicums or peppers. One is 'capsicum annum' which is the sweet pepper and the pepper variety used for Hungarian paprika. The other is 'capsicum frutescens', the hot pepper or chilli.

Europe quickly accepted the sweet pepper and it became a standard ingredient in Sofrito, a vegetable, meat and herb mixture which is the base of many Spanish dishes. It is also very popular in Italy and in Eastern Europe. Classic dishes include Piperade, Peperonata and stuffed peppers.

Peppers have only recently grown in popularity in the UK. They may be used raw in salads or cooked in stews, casseroles and stir-fry dishes.

Availability: All the year round.

Buying Guide: Choose fresh, bright specimens and check that they are firm throughout. The red and yellow peppers are riper and sweeter than the green ones.

Storage: Keep in the salad drawer of the fridge for two to three days. Green peppers will usually keep for longer than the others.

Preparation: Cut off the heads and scrape out the membranes and seeds from the centre. Slice or chop for use in salads.

Basic Cooking: Stuff and bake whole peppers in the oven or sauté and stew with onions or other vegetables and herbs. Use to flavour soups, casseroles, flans and stuffings.

STUFFED PEPPER RINGS [M]

Serve as part of a cold buffet or as a supper dish on their own with a green salad.

2 medium-sized green peppers
4 oz/100 g blue cheese
5 oz/150 g cream cheese
2 oz/50 g Cheddar cheese, grated
1 oz/25 g walnuts, chopped
freshly ground black pepper

Cut the heads of the top of the peppers and scrape out the seeds and membranes. Mix all the remaining ingredients together and stuff into the hollow peppers, pressing well down.

Place in the fridge and chill until the stuffing is firm. Cut the peppers horizontally into rings.

RED PEPPER GOUGÈRE [M]

If you cannot find red peppers, green ones can be used instead. The result will be as good but not so sweet.

1 large onion, sliced
1 tablespoon cooking oil
knob of butter
2 large red peppers, seeded and cut into strips
1 tablespoon tomato purée
1 large Continental tomato, peeled and chopped
1 tablespoon freshly chopped parsley

1 sprig rosemary or basil, freshly chopped
salt and freshly ground black pepper

Gougère
¼ pint/150 ml water
4 oz/100 g butter
4 oz/100 g plain flour
pinch salt
4 eggs
3 oz/75 g Gruyère cheese, grated
1 tablespoon grated Parmesan cheese

To prepare the filling, fry the onion in oil and butter until it turns transparent. Add the pepper strips and continue frying gently for a further 3—4 minutes. Add all the remaining filling ingredients and simmer for 20 minutes until thick and tender. Remove the lid and boil to reduce any excess liquid. Leave to cool.

To make the gougère, heat the water and butter in a saucepan. When the butter melts bring the mixture to the boil and beat in the flour and salt. Remove from the heat when the mixture starts to come away from the sides of the pan. Beat the eggs in, one at a time, and continue beating until the mixture is satin smooth.

Beat in the Gruyère cheese, and use the mixture to line an oval, heatproof entrée dish. Pile up the side and leave the centre base clear. Fill the hollow with the pepper mixture, sprinkle with Parmesan, and bake at 210°C/425°F/Gas 7 for 1 hour, 10 minutes. If necessary cover with foil for the last 15 minutes.

VEGETABLE AND SAUSAGE CRUMBLE   [M]

12 oz/350 g courgettes, sliced
1 oz/25 g butter
1 red pepper, seeded and chopped
1 green pepper, seeded and chopped
4 tomatoes, peeled and chopped
1 clove garlic, crushed
1 onion, chopped
salt and pepper
½ teaspoon mixed herbs
1 lb/450 g smoked pork sausages, sliced
4 oz/100 g Cheddar cheese, grated
2 oz/50 g fresh breadcrumbs

Cook the courgettes in boiling salted water for 4 minutes. Melt the butter in a frying pan and add the peppers, tomato, garlic and onion. Cook until soft. Season well and add the herbs.

Layer the courgettes, sausage slices and pepper and tomato mixture in an ovenproof dish. Sprinkle with cheese and breadcrumbs, then bake at 190°C/375°F/Gas 5 for 30—35 minutes.

CHINESE BEEF WITH PEPPERS [M]

Pork or lamb could be substituted for beef in this recipe. Make sure that all the ingredients are cut to similar lengths and thicknesses. This helps to ensure even cooking.

12 oz/350 g frying steak
cooking oil
1 tablespoon cornflour
1 tablespoon soy sauce
1 bunch spring onions, very finely chopped
1 large red pepper, seeded and cut into thin strips
1 large green pepper, seeded and cut into thin strips
pinch five-spice powder (optional)

Cut the steak very thinly across the grain and cut into pieces about 1½ in/4 cm in length. Toss in a little oil and then in cornflour.

Heat 2 tablespoons cooking oil in a wok or curved frying pan and stir-fry the beef for a minute. Add the soy sauce and continue sitr-frying for a further ½ minute. Remove from the pan and keep warm.

Add another 2 tablespoons of oil and stir-fry the spring onions and strips of pepper for a minute. Return the meat to the pan. Add the five-spice powder, if used. Toss over the heat and serve at once with Chinese noodles.

TEXAN RICE [A]

This recipe comes from a Texan friend who actually refers to this dish as Mexican rice. However, the genuine Mexican version is probably rather hotter than this mild but delicious dish.

2 tablespoons cooking oil
1 green chilli, seeded and finely chopped
pinch saffron
8 oz/225 g long-grain rice
1 x 14 oz/400 g can tomatoes
¼ pint/150 ml water
2 Spanish onions, cut into rings
1 red pepper, seeded and cut into rings
1 green pepper, seeded and cut into rings
salt and pepper

Heat the oil in a saucepan and fry the chilli and saffron for a minute or so. Add the rice and continue frying and stirring until it is very lightly browned. Add the contents of the can of tomatoes and the water. Stir once and bring to the boil. Arrange the onion and pepper slices on the top and season.

Cover with a lid and cook over a gentle heat for 30 minutes until the rice and vegetables are tender and all the liquid has been absorbed. Serve at once without stirring.

NEW POTATOES

These succulent young tubers are quite distinct from the maincrop varieties which appear later in the year (and see page 120 for more historical details about potatoes in general).

They were developed quite early on in the European life of the potato and 'new potatoes, new potatoes' was one of the cries of the nineteenth-century street sellers.

Availability: Small 'new' potatoes from Egypt and elsewhere appear in the shops just after Christmas but it is not really until the Jersey potatoes appear in late April that the *real* new potato is available. The British new potato season runs from late May until August.

Buying Guide: Choose samples from which you can rub the skin with your thumb. Look for any soil sticking to the skin — this should be damp. Avoid any which are turning green.

Storage: Eat as soon after purchase as possible. Keep in a cool, dark and airy place until needed.

Preparation: Scrub and cook in their skins or scrape off the skin.

Basic Cooking: Choose specimens which are all the same size and boil in lightly salted water until just tender. Add a little mint, parsley or other fresh herbs to the cooking water. Drain and toss in butter. For potato salad toss in mayonnaise or dressing while still warm and leave to cool. New potatoes can also be made into chips or be par-boiled and sautéed.

NEW POTATOES WITH BACON AND MINT   [A]

Serve as an accompaniment to a plain grilled or roasted meal, or as a main dish in its own right with green vegetables and carrots.

8 oz/225 g lean bacon, diced
1½ oz/40 g butter
1½ lb/700 g new potatoes, scrubbed
4 tablespoons freshly chopped mint
salt and black pepper

Fry the bacon in a non-stick frying pan to release some of the fat. Add the butter. Cut the potatoes into small dice but do not bother to peel them. Add to the pan and fry over a gentle heat for about 15 minutes until the potatoes are cooked through. Stir the pan and turn the potatoes fairly frequently. When the potatoes are cooked, stir in the mint and season to taste.

NEW POTATOES WITH CELERY   [A]

This is a fairly rich dish so serve with plainly grilled meat or fish.

1 lb/450 g new potatoes, scrubbed
6 large sticks celery, finely sliced
2 tablespoons yogurt
2 tablespoons mayonnaise
salt and black pepper
1 oz/25 g grated cheese

Boil the potatoes and celery in lightly salted water for 10—15 minutes until the vegetables are tender. Drain well. Add the yogurt, mayonnaise and seasoning and toss in the pan over a low heat. Do not allow the mixture to boil.

Transfer to a heatproof dish, sprinkle with cheese and brown under a hot grill for 2—3 minutes.

NEW POTATO CASSEROLE   [A]

I developed this idea when looking for ways of using up leftover Brie cheese from my last dinner party!

1½ lb/700 g new potatoes, boiled, skinned and sliced
6 oz/175 g button mushrooms, sliced
4 oz/100 g Brie, crusts removed and cut into slices
salt and pepper
¼ pint/150 ml double cream

Layer the potatoes, mushrooms and cheese in a heatproof entrée dish, sprinkling with salt and pepper as you go. Pour on the cream and bake at 200°C/400°F/Gas 6 for 30 minutes until lightly browned on top.

CARAMELISED POTATOES   [A]

In Denmark these potates are traditionally served with pork or game.

1½ lb/700 g small new potatoes, scrubbed
1 oz/25 g sugar
2 oz/50 g unsalted butter

Cook the potatoes in boiling salted water for about 10—12 minutes until tender, taking care to see that the skins do not split. Leave to cool a little, then skin.

Heat the sugar in a heavy based saucepan until it has melted and is golden in colour. Add the butter and stir until well mixed. Rinse the potatoes under the cold water tap and add to the pan. Cook over a gentle heat, turning the potatoes so that they are well coated with the caramel. Serve at once.

SWISS-STYLE POTATOES   [A]

This recipe was inspired by the Swiss raclette. In the French cantons of Switzerland, solid rounds of special cheese are toasted over an open flame and the melted cheese is served with freshly boiled potatoes in their skins.

1 lb/450 g small new potatoes, scrubbed
salt
4 oz/100 g Emmenthal cheese, cut into thin slices

Boil the potatoes in their skins in a little boiling salted water for 10—15 minutes until tender. Place in four heatproof dishes and cover with the slices of cheese. Place under a medium grill and serve as soon as the cheese melts, with cold ham and salad.

NEW POTATO SALAD WITH CRUSHED CARDAMOM
   DRESSING   [A]

In Eastern cooking, cardamoms are often used with milk-based products. The combination goes very well with new potatoes.

6 cardamom pods
8 oz/225 g yogurt
salt and pepper
1½ lb/700 g new potatoes, cooked and sliced

Remove the cardamom seeds from the pods and crush in a pestle and mortar. Mix with the yogurt and seasonings and pour over the sliced potatoes. Leave to stand in the fridge, well covered, for at least 2 hours before serving.

MANGETOUT

Sometimes known as sugar or sweet peas, mangetout look like flat peapods which have not fattened and this is indeed the case. The whole of the pod is eaten and it has a very sweet taste. Mangetout have been popular in France for some time but the British demand for them is growing every year. (See page 97 for some more historical details about peas in general.)

Availability: All the year round.

Buying Guide: Choose mangetout which are fresh and crisp with a good colour. Limp, pale specimens are showing their age. Avoid very large ones as they may be stringy.

Storage: Eat as soon after purchase as possible.

Preparation: Top, tail and string both sides of the pea and cook whole. Cut into strips for use in salads.

Basic Cooking: Steam in a steamer or boil in a very little salted boiling water for 5 minutes. Take care not to overcook or they will go flabby. Serve with butter and cream and summer savory. Alternatively stir-fry with herbs or with other vegetables.

SPAGHETTI WITH SAUTÉED SPRING VEGETABLES   [S]

This makes an unusual starter. Alternatively the quantities can be increased and the recipe served as a supper dish.

8 oz/225 g spaghetti
salt
olive oil
2—3 spring onions, finely chopped
2 new carrots, cut into sticks
6 oz/175 g mangetout, topped and tailed
2 oz/50 g peas
1 tablespoon freshly chopped parsley
4 tablespoons grated Parmesan cheese
freshly ground black pepper

Cook the spaghetti in plenty of salted boiling water together with a little olive oil. Follow the instructions on the pack and cook until just tender. Drain and toss in a little more olive oil. Keep warm.

Heat about 1½ tablespoons olive oil in a pan and sauté the spring onion and carrot sticks for 3—4 minutes. Add the mangetout and peas and continue cooking for a further 5 minutes until all the vegetables are tender and slightly crisp.

Pour over the spaghetti and sprinkle with parsley, cheese and black pepper. Serve at once.

STIR-FRY MANGETOUT WITH CHICKEN   [M]

Stir-fry dishes are best cooked in the traditional Chinese wok, but if this is not possible a large frying pan, preferably with curved edges, can be used. Be sure to keep the ingredients on the move and the oil as hot as you can get it.

8 spring onions, topped and halved
¼ in/5 mm ginger, very finely sliced (optional)
1 clove garlic, very finely chopped
4 tablespoons vegetable oil

8 oz/225 g chicken breast fillet, cut into thin strips
8 oz/225 g mangetout
3 oz/75 g peas, shelled weight
1 tablespoon soy sauce
1 tablespoon dry sherry

Fry the spring onion, ginger if used and garlic in 3 tablespoons vegetable oil for 1 minute. Add the chicken pieces and stir-fry for 1—2 minutes until all traces of pink have disappeared from the meat. Remove the chicken from the pan and keep on one side.

Add the remaining oil to the pan and stir-fry the mangetout and peas for 2 minutes. Return the chicken to the pan and add the soy sauce and sherry and stir until the sizzling stops and the chicken is heated through.

Serve with rice.

MANGETOUT AND ALMOND SALAD [A]

This salad is delicious served with cold roast lamb or with home-baked ham.

12 oz/350 g mangetout
2 tablespoons walnut oil
1 teaspoon lemon juice
1 oz/25 g walnuts, finely chopped
1 tablespoon freshly chopped parsley

Top, tail and string the mangetout and cut into long thin slices. Toss in nut oil with a very little lemon juice to taste. Sprinkle with walnuts and freshly chopped parsley just before serving.

JUNE

'There was an Old Person of Fife,
Who was greatly disgusted with life;
They sang him a ballad and fed him on salad,
Which cured that Old Person of Fife.'

Edward Lear (1812–1888)

Endive
Aubergines
Broad Beans
Cucumber

ENDIVE

There is some confusion over the name of this rather curly vegetable. On the Continent and in America, and in some cookery books, it is known as chicory. In the UK, it is endive or curly endive. It looks rather like a thin, crinkly-leaved lettuce and is used in much the same way.

The flavour of endive is slightly more bitter than lettuce and this probably reflects the much higher mineral content. It contains three times as much sodium and twice as much calcium and phosphorous. Sulphur and iron are also present along with all the vitamins usually found in green leaf vegetables.

Availability: All the year round but cheaper and more frequent during May to August.

Buying Guide: Choose fresh, crisp looking specimens and leave any which are withering at the edges.

Storage: Keep for a day or so in the salad compartment of the fridge.

Preparation: Cut off the base and separate the leaves. Wash very well in salted water. Use raw in salads.

Basic Cooking: Endive is usually eaten raw, but it can also be steamed and boiled like other green leaf vegetables.

CURLY ENDIVE AU GRATIN   [A]

This unusual recipe for cooking curly endive comes from Naples.

1 small head curly endive, washed and leaves separated
½ oz/15 g butter
salt
¼ pint/150 ml water
4 oz/100 g Cheddar cheese, grated
4 large tomatoes, peeled and chopped
1 tablespoon tomato purée
salt and pepper

Place the curly endive leaves in a saucepan with the butter, salt and water. Bring to the boil and cook fast for about 30 minutes until the endive is tender and most of the liquid has been used up.

Spoon into a greased casserole dish and sprinkle with half the cheese. Mix the chopped tomatoes with tomato purée and seasoning and spread over the endive and cheese. Add the remaining cheese and bake at 200°C/400°F/Gas 6 for 10—15 minutes.

CURLY ENDIVE SALAD [A]

I serve this as a side salad with plainly grilled meats such as steak or lamb chops. It also goes well with liver and bacon.

½ head curly endive, chopped
2 oz/50 g beansprouts, chopped
¼ green pepper, seeded and finely chopped
2 oz/50 g roasted peanuts, chopped
4 tablespoons quark low-fat soft cheese
1 tablespoon cider vinegar
1 oz/25 blue cheese, crumbled
milk

Mix the curly endive and beansprouts in a bowl. Sprinkle with green pepper and nuts.

Mix all the remaining ingredients together with a fork, adding sufficient milk to give a thick creamy consistency. Pour over the salad and serve.

FRENCH ENDIVE SALAD WITH POACHED EGG [A]

This is a variation on the previous recipe, which omits the peppers and the dressing.

Toss the endive and bean sprouts in a little olive oil and ground black pepper, and arrange in individual serving bowls. Add fried bread croûtons and crisply fried bacon bits and top with a lightly poached egg. Serve immediately.

AUBERGINES

Sometimes known as eggplants, these vegetables originated in Southern Asia and are now typical of the cooking of the Eastern Mediterranean.

Like tomatoes, aubergines belong to the nightshade family and at one time were referred to as 'mad apples' in the belief that they would cause insanity! Today aubergines must be one of the most popular vegetables in the world, for they are eaten in the Far and Near East, the Latin countries, the Americas and in Europe. Famous recipes using aubergines include Moussaka, Poor Man's Caviar, Imam Bayildi or Fainting Imam, and Ratatouille.

Availability: All the year round.

Buying Guide: Choose firm, smooth vegetables with a shine to them. Avoid any which are going wizened, have bruises or brown patches.

Storage: Store for two to three days in the salad compartment of the fridge.

Preparation: Wipe and trim both ends. There is no need to peel any but the oldest aubergines. Halve, slice or cube to cook. The bitter taste can be reduced by sprinkling with salt then leaving to stand for 30 minutes and rinsing in cold water. This treatment also cuts the water content and helps to stop the vegetable absorbing too much oil if it is to be fried.

Basic Cooking: Fry uncoated in oil, or coat with flour and egg, or batter. Cook with other vegetables such as onions and tomatoes or stuff and bake in the oven. Serve coated with cheese or in a cheese sauce.

AUBERGINE SALAD   [S]

This recipe originates in the Middle East where it may be served with grilled or roast meats. Try it as a starter with hot pitta bread.

2 aubergines
½ green pepper, seeded and finely chopped
2 tomatoes, peeled, seeded and chopped
½ small onion, finely chopped
1 clove garlic, crushed

1 teaspoon ground cumin
1 tablespoon freshly chopped parsley
2 teaspoons olive oil
juice of 1 lemon
salt and pepper

Bake aubergines in their skins in a hot oven, 200°C/400°F/Gas 6, until they feel soft to the touch and the skins have turned black (about an hour). Remove from the oven and leave to cool.

Scrape out all the flesh and chop finely. Mix with all the remaining ingredients, seasoning to taste.

Serve garnished with a little more chopped parsley.

AUBERGINE CASSEROLE   [M]

This is a Middle Eastern dish which is a main course in its own right.

4 eggs, beaten
3 tablespoons milk
4 oz/100 g Gruyère or Emmenthal cheese, grated
salt and black pepper
½ oz/15 g butter
4 tablespoons olive oil
2 aubergines, sliced
1 onion, finely chopped
2 tablespoons tomato purée
½ teaspoon dried marjoram
4 tomatoes, peeled and sliced
4—5 tablespoons freshly chopped parsley

Mix 2 eggs with 2 tablespoons of the milk and 3 tablespoons of the cheese. Season and pour into a soup bowl.

Heat half the butter and oil in a frying pan. Dip slices of aubergine in the egg mixture so that they are well coated all over and fry on both sides in the hot fat. Cook until well browned. Remove and keep on one side. Add more butter and oil as required and continue coating and frying until all the aubergines have been cooked.

Mix the remaining 2 eggs with the remaining 1 tablespoon of milk, onion, tomato purée and marjoram and season. Layer the cooked aubergines in a casserole with the sliced tomatoes, parsley, the remaining cheese and the egg mixture, ending with a layer of cheese. Bake at 190°C/375°F/Gas 5 for 45—50 minutes until the aubergines are soft.

Serve with a green salad and new potatoes.

SAUTÉED AUBERGINES [A]

This is a very simple but effective way to serve aubergines.

2 medium-sized aubergines
salt
1½ tablespoons olive oil
1 clove garlic, finely chopped
1 tablespoon basil or 2 tablespoons parsley or chervil, all freshly
  chopped
freshly ground black pepper

Cut the aubergines into ½ in/1 cm cubes. Sprinkle with salt and leave to drain for 30 minutes. Wash under cold water and squeeze out any excess liquid.

⌐ Separate the pieces of aubergine and fry in the olive oil in a heavy based frying pan with the garlic. Cook for 10 minutes, shaking the pan frequently so that the vegetables do not burn and cook evenly all over. Add the basil or parsley and black pepper and cook for a further 5 minutes.

AUBERGINE PILAU [A]

This dish comes from Saudi Arabia. It is excellent served with any kind of plain meat or with kebabs and salad.

¼ teaspoon whole mustard seeds or cumin seeds
½ teaspoon poppy seeds
2 whole cloves
½ teaspoon ground turmeric
¼ teaspoon ground cinnamon
1 tablespoon ground almonds
2 oz/50 g butter or 1 tablespoon oil and 1 oz/25 g butter
1 aubergine, peeled and diced
1 onion, finely chopped
8 oz/225 g long-grain rice
¾ pint/450 ml water
salt

Fry the spices and ground almonds in butter or a mixture of butter and oil. After a minute or so add the diced aubergine and stir well. Next add the onion and continue to fry gently for about 5 minutes, stirring regularly. Add the rice and stir well to make sure that the rice is well mixed in. Pour on the water and season. Bring to the boil and reduce the heat.

Cover and simmer for 15 minutes until the rice is tender and all the liquid has been absorbed. Turn off the heat and leave for 5 minutes. Fluff up the rice with a fork before serving.

BROAD BEANS

Broad beans are one of the oldest cultivated vegetables and they have been eaten in Britain for centuries. Very young beans can be eaten pod and all. Older specimens will need to be shelled before cooking.

Broad beans have been called by many names, including Horse Bean, Field Bean, Longpod and Windsor Bean. These beans were the food of the common people in Chaucer's time, and he referred to things as being 'not worth a bean'. Bacon was another staple food of the time and not surprisingly the two foods came to be eaten together. This association lasted for hundreds of years. Tradition has it that George III ate a breakfast of broad beans and bacon when he stopped for an impromptu meal with workmen building the Woolwich Arsenal.

Beans in parsley sauce with ham became a Victorian speciality and they are still served in the same way.

Availability: May to September.

Buying Guide: Choose pods which are fairly soft and tender but not limp.

Storage: Eat as soon as possible after purchase. Keep in a cool, dry place until needed.

Preparation: Top, tail and string very young beans and cut into lengths. Remove the beans from older pods and use in salads or cook.

Basic Cooking: Steam or boil shelled beans in lightly salted water for 15–20 minutes. Steam pods for 20–30 minutes. Serve with butter and savory or in a parsley cream sauce. Broad beans seem to go particularly well with egg dishes and with ham. Very old beans may be cooked and puréed or the skins may be removed by rubbing in a teacloth after boiling for a few minutes. Return the beans to the pan after removing the skins and continue cooking.

BROAD BEAN MOUSSE [S]

This attractive little starter is a good way of using up the larger and tougher beans.

12 oz/350 g shelled broad beans, cooked and cooled
1 egg, separated
3 tablespoons double cream, whisked
1 clove garlic, crushed
1 teaspoon Worcestershire sauce
½ teaspoon celery salt
salt and pepper
1 packet gelatine
2 tablespoons white wine or lemon juice
lemon slices, to garnish

Skin the beans and purée or sieve. Mix with the egg yolks, cream, garlic, Worcestershire sauce and season well with celery salt, salt and pepper.

Mix the gelatine with the wine or lemon juice in a cup and stand in a pan of hot water, stirring until the gelatine dissolves. Mix with the bean purée.

Stiffly whisk the egg whites and fold into the purée. Spoon the mixture into individual ramekin dishes and place in the fridge for at least 2 hours. Decorate with a thin slice of lemon and serve with brown bread.

BROAD BEAN AND BACON OMELETTE [M]

Broad beans seem to go very well with eggs. Here they are used to fill an omelette. This recipe is just sufficient for two people.

8 oz/225 g shelled broad beans
2 rashers streaky bacon, diced
4 eggs
2 tablespoons water

salt and freshly ground black pepper
knob of butter

Cook the broad beans in lightly salted boiling water for about 10—15 minutes until tender. Drain well. Dry-fry the streaky bacon in a non-stick frying pan until lightly browned. Add the beans to the pan and toss well together.

Beat the eggs, water and seasoning together with a fork. Melt the butter in an omelette pan and when it has heated up pour in the egg mixture. Stir into an omelette. Just before folding over, fill with the bean and bacon mixture.

BROAD BEANS IN LEMON SAUCE [A]

A deliciously simple sauce to go with broad beans.

1 lb/450 g shelled broad beans
¼ pint/150 ml dry white wine
2 tablespoons fresh lemon juice
2 teaspoons finely chopped onion
4 oz/100 g unsalted butter, cubed
1½ tablespoons double cream
salt and pepper

Boil the broad beans in a little boiling salted water for 10—15 minutes until tender.

Meanwhile, boil the white wine with the lemon juice and onions until the mixture is reduced to 3 tablespoons. Stir in the butter and add the double cream, a few blobs at a time, season to taste and pour over the beans.

BROAD BEANS PEASANT-STYLE [A]

I first tasted beans cooked in this manner in a small auberge *in the Auvergne. The proprietor was very cagey about the ingredients but this recipe is a good approximation!*

4 rashers streaky bacon, diced
1 small onion, very finely chopped
1 potato, peeled and diced
12 oz/350 g shelled broad beans
bouquet garni
4 tablespoons vegetable stock

Fry the bacon in a non-stick pan until the fat begins to run. Add the onion and potato and fry gently until the onion begins to change colour.

Add the remaining ingredients and bring to the boil. Reduce the heat a little and cook uncovered until the vegetables are tender and there is only a little liquid in the base of the pan.

CUCUMBER

For some reason Dr Johnson did not like cucumbers. He had this to say on the subject: 'A cucumber should be well sliced, and dressed with pepper and vinegar and then thrown out, as good for nothing'!

They were not too popular with Sir Compton Mackenzie either. He complained in an essay on teaparties about the sandwiches which were generally served. Cucumber sandwiches came in for the worst brickbat when he likened them to wet handkerchieves.

However, 'as cool as a cucumber' is the saying, and there is no doubt that they are very refreshing. Mostly eaten raw, they can also be salted and cooked.

Availability: All the year round.

Buying Guide: Select firm, straight cucumbers with a good colour. There are also some small ridged cucumbers available in the shops. These have a more bitter flavour and should be used in cooking, or pickled.

Storage: Keep in the salad compartment of the fridge or stem end down in a glass of cold water with the cut end covered in foil. Store in a cool, dark place.

Basic Cooking: Sprinkle with salt and leave to stand for 30 minutes. Wash and drain. Toss in flour and fry in butter with finely chopped shallots. Or boil and serve in a white sauce. Grate and use in mousses and soups.

CUCUMBER RING [S]

The Americans are very fond of jellied salads and this is a good example. Serve as a starter or as the centrepiece of a cold buffet.

4 oz/100 g cottage cheese
6 oz/175 g cream cheese
4 tablespoons mayonnaise
1 medium cucumber, grated
4 spring onions, finely chopped
4 medium stalks, celery, finely chopped
salt and pepper
½ oz/15 g packet gelatine
1 tablespoon lemon juice
2 tablespoons water
cucumber slices and radish flowers, to garnish

Mix the cottage and cream cheeses together and stir in the mayonnaise. Next add the vegetables and seasoning.

Dissolve the gelatine in the lemon juice and water in a cup placed in a pan of hot water. When the gelatine has dissolved completely add to the cucumber mixture.

Spoon into a 1 pint/600 ml ring mould and chill until set. Turn out to serve and garnish with cucumber slices and radish flowers.

WHITE FISH FILLETS WITH CUCUMBER [M]

This recipe was inspired by a meal at the Moulin de Mougin, the Michelin three-star restaurant run by Roger Vergé near Cannes in the South of France. His recipe was rather more elaborate, but this still makes an excellent entrée.

4 fillets of white fish such as haddock, whiting or turbot (about
    1½ lb/700 g)
4—5 in/10—12.5 cm cucumber
1½ oz/40 g softened butter
salt and pepper
2 fl. oz/50 ml double cream, whipped with a fork until fairly stiff

Trim the fillets and arrange on a wire rack. Run a fork down the skin of the cucumber, and do this all the way round. Slice very thinly. Brush the top of the fish with plenty of butter and sprinkle with salt and pepper. Arrange the cucumber slices in lightly overlapping rows on top of the fish and brush with a little more butter.

Place the rack over an entrée dish or baking tin filled with boiling water. Place in the centre of the oven set to 200°C/400°F/Gas 6 and cook for 10—15 minutes until the fish is just tender. Carefully transfer to warmed plates and pipe a mound of cream on top of each fillet. Serve at once.

GRATIN OF CUCUMBER, PRAWNS AND EGGS [M]

This is another French inspired recipe. It makes an excellent light lunch or supper dish.

4 small ridge cucumbers or 2 smooth cucumbers
6 tablespoons white wine
4 oz/100 g button mushrooms, sliced
1 oz/25 g butter
4 oz/100 g peeled prawns
3 hard-boiled eggs, cut into quarters
salt and pepper
2 egg yolks
¼ pint/150 ml double cream, lightly whisked

Peel the cucumbers and cut into thick slices. Place in a saucepan with the white wine and bring to the boil. Cook for about 12 minutes until the cucumbers are tender. Remove the cucumbers to the base of a gratin dish and keep warm. Reserve the wine juice.

Very gently fry the mushrooms in the butter. When they are just softened, sprinkle over the cucumbers, then add the prawns, egg quarters and seasoning. Continue to keep warm.

Pour the cucumber/wine juice into the mushroom pan and bring to the boil. Beat the egg yolks into the cream and add the mixture to the pan. Continue beating with a whisk until the mixture thickens a little. Pour over the cucumbers, prawns and eggs and place under a hot grill until a golden skin forms over the top. Serve at once.

SCALLOPED CHICKEN AND CUCUMBER [M]

Serve as a lunch or supper dish or use smaller quantities and serve as a starter.

2 oz/50 g butter
1 tablespoon cooking oil
8 oz/225 g button mushrooms, sliced thickly and cut into sticks
1 small or ½ large cucumber, cut into sticks
¼ teaspoon garlic salt
¼ teaspoon dried thyme
12 oz/350 g cooked chicken meat, shredded
1 tablespoon soy sauce
¼ pint/150 ml double cream
black pepper
2 oz/50 g fresh breadcrumbs

Heat 1 oz/25 g of the butter with the oil in a pan and gently fry the mushrooms for 2—3 minutes. Add the cucumber, garlic salt and thyme and continue frying for a further 2—3 minutes. Add all the remaining ingredients except the breadcrumbs and bring to the boil. Cook for 2—3 minutes to thicken the sauce a little.

Transfer to four scallop shells. Sprinkle with breadcrumbs and dot with the remaining butter. Brown quickly under a hot grill.

RAITA   [A]

This cooling yogurt dish goes well with both Indian and Middle Eastern dishes. In the latter area garlic is added instead of cumin seeds, and the dish is served as an appetiser with hot pitta bread.

8 oz/225 g plain yogurt
4 in/10 cm cucumber, diced or coarsely grated
2 tablespoons freshly chopped mint
½ teaspoon ground cumin
¼ teaspoon cayenne pepper
salt

Whisk the yogurt to make it really smooth and stir in all the other ingredients. Chill before serving.

JULY

'Lettuce, like conversation, requires a good deal of oil, to avoid friction and to keep the company smooth.'

Charles Dudley Warner (1871)

Lettuce
Fennel
French Beans
Peas

LETTUCE

It is not known when lettuces were first introduced into Britain but they are mentioned in a fifteenth-century book on gardening. At that time they were more likely to be cooked with other 'pot herbs' or green vegetables than eaten raw. In Elizabethan times lettuce had a reputation for being an aphrodisiac but this viewpoint seems to have disappeared since then!

There are various types of lettuce available and these include the crisp, round Webb's Wonder types and tightly-hearted Icebergs; the soft round cabbages and the unhearted butterflies; and the long-leaved Cos.

Availability: At least one or two varieties will be on sale at any time of the year.

Buying Guide: Whatever the kind of lettuce it should be fresh with a good colour and no discoloured leaves or sliminess. Avoid those with the outside leaves removed.

Storage: Store in the salad drawer of the fridge or wrap in damp newspaper and keep in a saucepan in a cool place.

Preparation: Trim the base and any tough outer leaves. Wash whole for braising or baking and blanch in boiling water for a minute or two before cooking. Refresh in cold water. Otherwise separate the leaves and wash in salted water. Handle carefully as the leaves are easily damaged. Tear into pieces for salads or shred with a knife for garnish.

Basic Cooking: Fry a little onion, carrot and bacon in butter. Fold the lettuce into shapes and lay on the vegetables. Add a little stock, cover and cook for 40 minutes. Alternatively steam and serve with a cheese sauce. Use in soups.

CHILLED LETTUCE AND YOGURT SOUP   [S]

I used Cos lettuce for this recipe but any kind of lettuce can be cooked in this way. This soup serves six people.

1 onion, sliced
2 tablespoons cooking oil
2 fl. oz/50 ml dry sherry
1 Cos lettuce, shredded
1¼ pints/750 ml vegetable or chicken stock
salt and pepper
5 oz/150 g natural yogurt
pinch dried rosemary or tarragon

Gently fry the onion in cooking oil until lightly browned. Add the sherry and bring to the boil. Add the lettuce and stock and return to the boil. Season and simmer for 20 minutes. Purée in a blender or sieve. Leave to cool.

When cold whisk in the yogurt with a wire whisk, add the rosemary or tarragon and correct the seasoning if necessary. Chill for an hour before serving.

LETTUCE, CHEESE AND HAM PANCAKES [M]

These pancakes are based on a Swedish recipe.

8 medium-sized pancakes

Filling
¼ of an Iceberg lettuce, finely shredded
6 oz/175 g Gruyère cheese, grated
1 tablespoon grated onion
1 teaspoon French mustard
2 tablespoons coarsely chopped parsley
1 egg, beaten
salt
freshly ground black pepper
8 thin slices ham
¼ pint/150 ml double cream
1 tablespoon grated Parmesan cheese

To make the filling, mix the shredded lettuce with the Gruyère cheese (saving 2 tablespoons) and the grated onion. Mix the mustard with the parsley and the beaten egg and add salt and pepper to taste, then stir into the lettuce mixture.

Lay the pancakes out flat and lay a slice of ham on top of each one. Divide the lettuce and cheese filling between the pancakes and roll each one up. Place in a greased shallow ovenproof dish, spoon the double cream evenly over the top and sprinkle with the reserved Gruyère and the Parmesan. Bake at 190°C/375°F/Gas 5 for about 20 minutes. Serve piping hot.

LETTUCE WITH PEAS   [A]

Lettuce cooked with peas is part of the classic French cuisine. Here spring onions add a little more piquancy.

1 medium-sized Webb's hearted lettuce
1 bunch spring onions, trimmed
6 oz/175 g shelled peas
knob of butter
1—2 sugar lumps
3 tablespoons water
2 sprigs parsley

Cut the lettuce into quarters, wash and drain very well. Place all the ingredients in a saucepan and bring to the boil. Cover and reduce the heat. Cook very gently for about 20 minutes until all the vegetables are tender.

Transfer to a warmed serving dish. Remove the sprigs of parsley and serve at once.

BRAISED LETTUCE WITH APPLE   [A]

This is one of my favourite lettuce recipes. Serve it with roast pork or grilled pork chops.

1 oz/25 g butter
1 Cos lettuce, washed, outer leaves removed
1 cooking apple, peeled, cored and sliced thinly
juice of 1 lemon

Melt the butter in a pan. Shred the lettuce and sauté gently for 2—3 minutes. Add the apple and lemon juice and leave to simmer for 15—20 minutes. Stir once with a fork and serve with roast pork or duck.

FENNEL

There are two distinct varieties of fennel: the bulbous, celery-like vegetable with a pronounced aniseed flavour, sometimes known as Italian or Florence fennel; and the herb fennel. This latter was popular with the Romans and they are credited with introducing it to Britain, where it became well established in cookery before the Norman Conquest. (Much later it was taken to California and it is now one of their most common weeds.)

Fennel and fish go well together and this combination was well exploited on the many medieval feast days. It was also used with pork. The use of fennel herb with fish has remained a Mediterranean speciality but is not so well known here. The Italians also use fennel seed in many of their flavouring mixes.

The large bulbous root is also used extensively on the Continent, and is gaining in popularity in the UK.

Availability: July to March.

Buying Guide: Buy specimens with crisp and fleshy outside leaves. Avoid those which are at all brown or shrivelled.

Preparation: Cut off the base and stalks, retaining any green feathery shoots for flavouring. Remove stringy leaves and shred for salads or quarter or slice to cook.

Storage: Store in the salad compartment of the fridge for up to a week.

Basic Cooking: Steam in a steamer or in a very little salted water for about 15 minutes until tender. Do not boil in a lot of water or it will lose its flavour. Toss in butter or serve in a white or cheese sauce. Braise as for celery. Use to flavour soups and casseroles.

CHILLED FENNEL SOUP [S]

The use of fennel herb has a surprisingly long history in the UK and this recipe is based on one which was popular in the fourteenth century, but, as the flavours are very similar, the root is used instead of the herb.

1 large head fennel, trimmed
¾ pint/450 ml water
4 fl. oz/100 dry white wine
salt and pepper
1 oz/25 g ground almonds
5 oz/150 g plain yogurt

Retain a little of the feathery green parts of the head of fennel and coarsely chop the rest. Place in a pan with the water, wine and seasonings. Bring to the boil, cover and simmer for 30 minutes.

Sieve the soup or process in a food processor. Return to the pan and stir in the ground almonds. Return to the boil and simmer for a further 15 minutes, stirring from time to time. Remove from the heat and leave to cool.

Mix in the yogurt and chill for at least 30 minutes before serving. Finely chop the green feathery parts and sprinkle over the soup.

FENNEL AND TUNA SALAD [S]

I picked this recipe up on a holiday in southern Italy. There they used fresh tuna, but canned tuna is almost as good.

2 heads Italian fennel
salt
4 oz/100 g shelled broad beans
1 x 7 oz/200 g can tuna in brine, flaked
4 spring onions, very finely chopped
1 tablespoon freshly chopped parsley
2 tablespoons salad oil
2 teaspoons fresh lemon juice
black pepper

Trim the fennel and cut into quarters. Cook in a very little salted water for 10 minutes. Drain and coarsely chop. Cook the broad beans until tender in salted water. Drain and leave to cool. Mix fennel with the beans and spread over a small serving plate.

Mix the tuna, spring onions and parsley and pile over the centre of the fennel and bean mixture. Mix the salad oil with lemon juice and seasonings and pour all over the salad. Chill for 15—20 minutes and serve.

FENNEL SOUFFLÉS [A]

These delicate vegetable moulds can also be made with carrot or celeriac in place of fennel. Serve as a starter with a fresh tomato sauce (see page 46) or as an accompaniment to roast and grilled meats.

2 large heads Italian fennel, trimmed
2 eggs, beaten
1 tablespoon plain flour
2 fl. oz/50 ml milk
salt and pepper

Cut the fennel into pieces and cook in lightly salted boiling water for about 10 minutes until tender. Drain well on kitchen paper. Chop very finely or process in a food processor.

Mix with all the remaining ingredients and pour into four well greased ramekin or individual soufflé dishes. Place on a roasting tin with 1 in/2.5 cm hot water in the base and bake at 190°C/375°F/ Gas 5 for 50—60 minutes until the centres are firm and the tops lightly browned. Turn out to serve.

FRENCH BEANS

Gerard's *Herball* of 1597 refers to these beans as Brazil kidney beans, and they do come from South America, but more probably from Peru than Brazil. They were introduced to the UK from France, hence their modern name.

French beans are usually eaten when they are very young and they therefore do not need stringing. When mature, the pods are discarded and the beans dried for haricot beans.

Availability: June to September. Hot-house varieties are available, at a price, for most of the year.

Buying Guide: Beans should be fresh and juicy and snap easily between the fingers. The finer and thinner the beans the more expensive they will be.

Storage: Eat as soon as possible after purchase. Keep in a cool, dry place until needed.

Preparation: Wash and top and tail. String older beans. Chop for use in salads.

Basic Cooking: Cook whole in a little salted boiling water for about 5—10 minutes until only just tender. Serve with a little butter flavoured with garlic, fresh herbs or tomato. Serve cold with a vinaigrette sauce and in mixed salads such as Salade Niçoise.

BEANS AND FISH TERRINE   [S]

Serve this colourful terrine cut into slices, which shows off the layers to best advantage. Serve with a little cold tomato sauce (see page 46) and with Melba toast.

8 oz/225 g French beans, topped and tailed
1 lb/450 g white fish fillets, skinned
2 oz/50 g fresh breadcrumbs
4 tablespoons double cream
2 tablespoons dry vermouth
2 tablespoons lemon juice
1 egg, beaten
salt and pepper

Steam the beans in a steamer or in a very little boiling salted water until just tender. Drain and leave to cool. Chop the fish into small pieces and remove any stray bones. Mince the fish or process it in a food processor with the remaining listed ingredients.

Butter a pâté dish and place a third of the fish mixture in the base. Smooth it out flat. Arrange half the beans lengthways on the top. Cover with another third of the fish mixture, then the rest of the beans, finishing with a final layer of fish.

Cover with foil and place in a baking tin filled with 1 in/2.5 cm hot water. Bake at 180°C/350°F/Gas 4 for 1 hour. Pour off any liquid and run round the sides with a flat knife and leave to cool. Chill slightly and turn out. Serve in slices.

FRENCH BEAN AND LAMB MARENGO [M]

*All this rich lamb and bean stew needs to complete the meal is a
bowl of rice. Try a little garlic as an optional extra.*

½ oz/15 g butter
1½ lb/700 g lean lamb, cut into cubes
2 onions, thickly sliced
2 tablespoons tomato purée
salt and freshly ground black pepper
½ teaspoon ground coriander
pinch chilli powder or a few drops Tabasco sauce
1 lb/450 g French beans, topped and tailed
2 cloves
3 tomatoes, coarsely chopped
¼ pint/150 ml water
1 tablespoon lemon juice

Heat the butter in a large saucepan and fry the meat and onions
until the meat is well sealed. Add the tomato purée, seasonings
and spices and stir well. Cook over a low heat for 10 minutes,
stirring from time to time.

Add all the remaining ingredients except the lemon juice. Bring
to the boil and simmer for 1 hour until the meat is tender. Add
the lemon juice and cook uncovered for a further 15 minutes.

BEAN AND CUMIN PIE [M]

*If possible use an old-fashioned straight-sided fairly deep flan tin
for this pie.*

1 teaspoons whole cumin seeds
1 tablespoon cooking oil
knob of butter
1 onion, sliced
1 stick celery, finely chopped
8 oz/225 g French beans, topped, tailed and cut in half
14 oz/400 g shortcrust pastry
2 eggs
3 tablespoons double cream
5 tablespoons milk
salt and pepper

Fry the cumin seeds in the oil and butter for about a minute until they start to brown. Add the onion and celery and fry gently until the onion turns transparent. Add the beans and fry gently, stirring all the time for about 5 minutes until the beans begin to soften.

Roll out the pastry and use two-thirds to line an 8 in/20 cm straight-sided flan tin. Spoon in the bean and cumin mixture. Mix all the remaining ingredients together and pour over the vegetables.

Roll out the rest of the pastry and cut a round which will just fit inside the top of the flan. Prick well with a fork and lay on top of the flan. Fold the sides of the lower piece of pastry over the top, crimping into a pattern. Bake at 190°C/375°F/Gas 5 for 1 hour. Serve hot or cold.

GREEN BEANS WITH ORANGE AND ALMONDS [A]

This treatment gives a slightly different slant to plain green beans. Serve with a rich beef casserole or with roast duck or goose.

1 lb/450 g French beans, topped and tailed
salt and black pepper
juice and rind of ½ orange
1 tablespoon orange juice
1 oz/25 g butter
2 tablespoons flaked almonds, toasted under the grill

Cook the beans in a very little lightly salted water until just tender. This will take about 5—8 minutes depending on their size.

Drain well and add all the remaining ingredients except the almonds. Bring to the boil and continue boiling until almost all the liquid has been taken up. Sprinkle with toasted almonds and serve.

COLD BEAN SALAD [A]

Try this salad with a tomato dressing or with an unusual peanut butter sauce.

1 lb/450 g French beans, topped and tailed
salt and black pepper
4 tablespoons tomato juice
2 tablespoons salad oil
1 tablespoon lemon juice
½ teaspoon sugar
1 clove garlic, crushed
1 tablespoon finely chopped onion or shallot

Cook the beans in very little boiling salted water until just tender. Drain and leave to cool.

Mix the remaining ingredients and beat with a fork. Pour over the beans and chill for about an hour, then serve.

GREEN BEAN SALAD WITH PEANUT BUTTER DRESSING [A]

In place of the tomato dressing above, dilute 2 tablespoons smooth peanut butter with milk to make a cream. Add 1 tablespoon vinegar or lemon juice, a clove of crushed garlic and, if you have it, a little grated fresh root ginger, and pour over the beans as before.

PEAS

The fresh peas we know today are a much finer variety than those which fed our ancestors. Split and dried peas were the order of the day for medieval man, and indeed for the Greeks and Romans. But they were very popular, so much so that at some political elections in Rome they were issued free in return for a vote!

It is rare these days to find good fresh peas since so many of them go to the frozen food manufacturers. However, young peas fresh from the pod are really worth looking for.

Availability: May to September, peaking in July.

Buying Guide: Look for pods which are not too full and avoid wet pods. Good peas should disintegrate under gentle finger and thumb pressure. Allow about 1½ lb/700 g peas in their pods to yield ¾ lb/350 g shelled peas.

Superstition has it that pods filled with either one or nine peas are lucky. Throw one of the peas over your right shoulder and make a wish!

Storage: Eat as soon as possible after purchase, or shell and store in a polythene bag in the fridge for a day or so.

Preparation: Shell and eat raw in salads.

Basic Cooking: Boil with a sprig of mint and a little sugar and salt for about 15 minutes until tender. Steam for about 20 minutes. Serve with a knob of butter. Use in soups and casseroles; add to the latter about 15 minutes before the end of the cooking time. Peas also make a pretty garnish for cold flans and salads. Old peas are best cooked and puréed with a little butter and cream.

GREEN VELVET SOUP   [S]

This amazingly economical soup actually uses the pods left after shelling peas!

1 large onion, sliced
1 oz/25 g butter
1 large potato, peeled and sliced
pods from 1 lb/450 g peas, washed
1¼ pints/750 ml chicken stock
¼ pint/150 ml milk
salt and pepper

Gently fry the onion in butter until it turns transparent. Add the potato, pea pods and chicken stock and bring to the boil. Simmer, covered, for 30 minutes. Liquidise in a blender or food processor and then sieve to remove the fibres.

Return the purée to the pan, stir in the milk and season to taste. Bring to the boil again and serve. It looks quite pretty to float a few cooked peas in the soup if you have them.

FRICASSÉE OF FRESH PEAS WITH SWEETBREADS   [M]

This is a favourite of mine for really special dinner parties. Serve with new potatoes.

1½ lb/700 g lamb's sweetbreads
1 carrot, thickly sliced
1 onion, quartered
1 bouquet garni
milk
4 oz/100 g butter
2 oz/50 g plain flour
8 oz/225 g fresh peas
salt and pepper
4 slices white bread
8 short rashers streaky bacon
3 tablespoons double cream

1 teaspoon lemon juice
¼ teaspoon ground mace or grated nutmeg.

Soak the sweetbreads in cold water for 3 hours, changing the water once. Drain and place in a pan with fresh water. Bring to the boil and simmer for 3—4 minutes. Drain and plunge into cold water. Remove any skin and pieces of sinew or gristle, and cut into pieces. Place in a pan with the carrot, onion and bouquet garni. Cover with ¾ pint/450 ml water. Bring to the boil and simmer for 15 minutes.

Remove the vegetables and discard. Remove the sweetbreads and keep on one side. Boil up the liquid for a further 5 minutes and then make up to 1 pint/600 ml with milk. Melt 2 oz/50 g of the butter in another pan and add the flour and the milk mixture. Bring to the boil, stirring all the time. Add the peas and seasoning and simmer for 10 minutes, stirring from time to time.

Fry the bread in the remaining butter until crisp and golden and cut into triangles. Roll up the bacon rashers and grill.

Add the cream, lemon juice and mace or nutmeg to the peas and sauce. Return to the boil and add the sweetbreads. Heat through and correct the seasoning. Serve garnished with fried bread triangles and bacon rolls.

CURRIED RICE WITH PEAS [A]

Rice and peas is a traditional combination throughout Latin America and the Caribbean. The addition of curry in this recipe gives a lift to an old favourite.

8 oz/225 g long-grain rice
2 teaspoons mild curry powder
4 oz/100 g frozen peas, thawed
1 x 10 fl. oz/300 ml can condensed consommé
6 fl. oz/175 ml water
salt and pepper

Mix the rice with the curry powder and place in a casserole. Stir in the peas. Heat the consommé and water and pour over the rice mixture. Sprinkle with salt and pepper.

Cover and bake at 180°C/350°F/Gas 4 for about 45 minutes until all the liquid has been absorbed and the rice is tender. Fluff up with a fork before serving.

INDIAN KEEMA CURRY   [M]

The Keema curry traditionally uses peas. Here I have used fresh peas, but frozen peas work just as well out of season.

3 tablespoons vegetable oil
1 large onion, finely chopped
3 cloves garlic, peeled and chopped
1 lb/450 g raw minced lamb or beef
1 in/2 cm piece of root ginger, peeled and grated
1 tablespoon ground cumin
1 tablespoon ground coriander
salt and pepper
¼ pint/150 ml water
8 oz/225 g shelled peas
3—4 tablespoons freshly chopped green coriander
1 teaspoon garam masala or curry powder
juice of ½ lemon
3 tomatoes, quartered

Heat the oil in a pan and fry the onion and garlic until lightly browned. Add the lamb or beef and stir well. Add the ginger, spices and seasonings and cook until the meat is browned all over.

Pour on the water and bring to the boil. Simmer for 30 minutes.

Skim off any excess fat and add all the remaining ingredients except the tomatoes. Stir and return to the boil. Place the tomato quarters on the top. Cover and simmer for another 10 minutes. Serve with rice.

AUGUST

'There was an Old Man of Orleans,
Who was given to eating of beans,
Till once out of sport, he swallowed a quart,
That dyspeptic Old Man of Orleans.'

Edward Lear (1812—1888)

Globe Artichokes
Beetroot
Runner Beans
Broccoli and Calabrese

GLOBE ARTICHOKES

This thistle-like plant has been cultivated for so many centuries that it has improved beyond recognition. In the Middle Ages and during the Renaissance, it gained something of a scandalous reputation for being an aphrodisiac, which may account for why it was considered most improper for gentlewomen to be seen eating them.

The only edible parts of the artichoke are the basal tips of the stubby leaves and the bottom or fond which is hidden beneath the choke of almost hair-like growth.

Herbalists in the Middle Ages ascribed all kinds of qualities to globe artichokes, which included curing unmentionable diseases, reducing fever and stimulating the appetite. More recently, extracts from artichokes were used in the treatment of liver disorders.

Availability: May to September.

Buying Guide: There are two types — purple and green — but there is no difference in the way they are treated and cooked. Globe artichokes should be firm with stiff leaves that have a slight bloom to them. Avoid those which have the leaves fully open or which look discoloured.

Storage: Cook on day of purchase or cut off a little of the stem and stand in water overnight.

Preparation: Wash well in salted water. Knock off the stalk by hitting with a rolling pin. This method of removing the stalk pulls out most of the stiff spines which can mar the heart. Snip off the points of the leaves with a pair of scissors (this is actually more cosmetic than necessary). If only the hearts are required cut off the leaves with a sharp knife and then scoop out the choke with a teaspoon.

This choke also needs to be removed from whole cooked artichokes. To do this open out the leaves on the top and pull out the small ones in the centre which have no flesh on their ends. Carefully scoop out the choke by easing away from the heart with a fork.

Basic Cooking: Plunge whole artichokes into boiling salted water to which has been added the juice of a lemon and the squeezed halves. Cover and boil for about 40 minutes until the leaves easily come away on pulling. Remove the choke and serve hot or cold with drawn butter, hollandaise sauce or vinaigrette. Boil hearts in the same way for 15 minutes and use to garnish salads. Alternatively fry in batter or fill with puréed or diced vegetables and serve with the main course. Use in flans.

BRIARDE DRESSING FOR ARTICHOKES   [S]

This is my favourite dressing for those large French artichokes. Its fresh and piquant flavour seems to go very well with that of the artichoke. I worked it out in France using fromage blanc, but quark works just as well.

8 oz/225 quark low-fat soft cheese
2 tablespoons milk or water
1 tablespoon red wine vinegar
4—5 radishes, finely chopped
3—4 gherkins, finely chopped
1 tablespoon freshly chopped basil
salt and black pepper

Blend the quark, milk or water and vinegar to a smooth cream. Stir in all the remaining ingredients and serve with cold cooked globe artichokes.

STUFFED ARTICHOKES   [S]

If you are planning to serve only the base of the artichoke it is better to cut it out before cooking as described below. This results in a larger base as some of the flesh from the bottom of the leaves is left behind on the base.

4 artichokes
1 lemon, quartered
2 oz/50 g quark low-fat soft cheese
1 cooked salmon steak, flaked
1 tablespoon freshly chopped dill or ½ teaspoon dried
salt and black pepper
4 sprigs parsley
4 thin slices of lemon

Knock off the stems of the artichokes and peel round the outside with a very sharp knife to cut off all the leaves. Work upwards until all the leaves have been removed and only the fonds and chokes are left. Carefully scoop the chokes out with a small melon baller or parisienne potato cutter, taking care not to take too much of the base with the choke.

Drop bases into water with the lemon, and bring to the boil. Simmer for about 15 minutes until the bases are tender. Leave to cool.

Carefully mix the quark with the flaked salmon, dill and seasonings. Spoon the mixture onto the cold artichoke bases and pile up. Decorate each with a sprig of parsley and a lemon butterfly.

BEETROOT

Beetroot is one of the most under-rated of our root vegetables. It is available almost all the year round yet it only occasionally appears on our tables in a salad or pickled in vinegar to accompany cold meats. Other countries have appreciated its culinary value much more, using it in classic dishes as varied as Borsch and Scandinavian meatballs.

Young beetroot is available in bunches with the leaves still attached and these leaves can be cooked as a vegetable in their own right. Older beetroot may be sold cooked or uncooked. It can be eaten raw or it can be cooked and eaten either hot or cold.

Availability: All the year round.

Buying Guide: All uncooked beetroot should be firm and fresh and not too large. The foliage of bunched beetroot should be crisp and fresh. Cooked beetroot should be a rich, bright colour and have skins which rub off easily.

Storage: Store uncooked beetroot in a cool, dark, dry and airy place. Cooked beetroot should be stored in the fridge or cold larder for a few days only. Cooked beetroot may also be skinned and sliced and stored covered in vinegar.

Preparation: Take care not to remove the stalks or roots from uncooked beetroot too near to the tuber or it will 'bleed' and lose its colour. Scrub and cook in its skin. Peel and grate for salads.

Basic Cooking: Boil in plenty of salted boiling water for 40—60 minutes. Larger specimens may take longer. Avoid too much prod-ding with a fork. Alternatively bake in a covered container or in foil for about the same length of time. Once cooked and peeled, the beetroot may be sliced or diced and served hot with cream or in an orange sauce. Serve cold in salads.

BORSCH

This smooth version of the traditional Russian Borsch is perfect to serve at a dinner party.

1 medium onion, finely chopped
1 oz/25 g butter
3 medium-sized cooked beetroots, skinned and roughly chopped
1 clove garlic, crushed
1 pint/600 ml chicken stock
salt and pepper
¼ pint/150 ml soured cream

Fry the onion gently in the butter until softened, but not coloured. Add the beetroot, garlic, stock, salt and pepper, and simmer for 5 minutes. Liquidise until smooth and allow to cool. Chill for at least 4 hours.

Before serving, stir in the soured cream carefully to achieve a marbled effect.

FINNISH BEETBURGERS   [M]

This is a popular variation on the standard beefburgers in all the Scandinavian countries.

1¼ lb/575 g lean beef, minced
1 small onion, finely chopped
6 oz/175 g cooked beetroot, finely diced
1 tablespoon mayonnaise
½ teaspoon dried dill
pinch ground nutmeg
salt and pepper
a little butter

Place all the ingredients, except the butter, in a bowl and mix well together with a fork. It may take some time until all the beet-root stays in the mixture.

Shape into four large hamburgers and fry in a knob of butter for about 4–5 minutes on each side depending on how well cooked you like your burgers.

STEWED BEETROOT WITH ONIONS [A]

Beetroot is one of my favourite vegetables, and I particularly like it hot. This recipe is quite spicy, and goes well with lamb and beef casseroles, and with grilled meats.

2 tablespoons cooking oil
1 teaspoon whole cumin seeds
1 clove garlic, peeled and crushed
2 onions, sliced
salt and black pepper
4 small raw beetroot (1 lb/450 g), peeled and cut into wedges
2 tablespoons tomato purée
juice of 1 lemon
4 fl. oz/100 ml water

Heat the cooking oil in a pan and fry the cumin seeds and garlic for 1 minute. Add the onion and fry for a further 2–3 minutes. Then add all the remaining ingredients.

Bring to the boil and simmer, covered, for 50 minutes or until the beetroot is tender. Stir from time to time.

BEETROOT IN ORANGE [A]

This recipe has a more delicate flavour than the previous one, and is suitable for serving with chicken or even with fish.

½ oz/15 g butter
1 bunch spring onions, chopped
1 lb/450 g cooked beetroot, diced
2 fl. oz/50 ml orange juice
black pepper

Melt the butter in a pan and gently fry the spring onions until they begin to soften. Add the beetroot and toss the mixture well together. Pour on the orange juice.

Turn up the heat and cook for about 10 minutes, stirring fairly frequently, until all the liquid has disappeared. Serve at once sprinkled with freshly ground black pepper.

BEETROOT AND CUCUMBER SALAD [A]

This makes a change from the usual beetroot in vinegar. It is also reputed to be the chosen accompaniment to roast grouse in Scottish country houses.

2 medium-sized beetroot, cooked and peeled
3 in/7.5 cm piece cucumber
2 tablespoons salad oil
1 tablespoon lemon juice
1 tablespoon freshly chopped parsley (optional)
freshly ground black pepper

Slice the beetroot and cucumber fairly thinly. Arrange the sliced vegetables alternately in a spiral pattern on four individual salad dishes.

Mix the oil and lemon juice and pour over the salad. Sprinkle with parsley, if used, and freshly ground black pepper.

RUNNER BEANS

This very British bean actually comes from South America and, like the tomato plant, was originally grown as an ornamental climbing plant. It was not until the nineteenth century that runner beans were grown for their food value. However, once on the British market, they quickly took over from other types of beans.

They grow much larger than the French bean but can still remain crisp and tender. However, they need to have their stringy sides removed.

Availability: Mid July to autumn.

Buying Guide: A good bean should look fresh and break crisply. Avoid over-large or very curly beans for they are likely to be particularly tough and stringy.

Storage: Eat as soon as possible after purchase. Keep in a cool dry place until needed.

Preparation: Top and tail and string the beans. Slice to eat raw or to cook.

Basic Cooking: Boil or steam in a very little water. Add fresh or dried savory for extra flavour. Toss in butter or serve with tomato and garlic sauce.

MIMOSA SALAD   [S]

Use young tender runner beans for the recipe and cook them whole.

1 lb/450 g young runner beans, topped, tailed and stringed
salt
4 tablespoons olive oil
1 tablespoon lemon juice
freshly ground black pepper
2 hard-boiled eggs

Steam the beans in a steamer or in a very little salted water until just tender. Drain and leave to cool a little. Mix the olive oil and lemon juice and pour over the beans while they are still warm. Leave to cool completely.

Arrange the beans in a star shape with the ends into the centre on a round plate. Sprinkle with black pepper.

Rub the egg yolks through a sieve and finely chop the egg whites. Pile the latter in the centre of the dish and use the sieved yolks to make star rays along five or six lines of beans.

RUNNER BEAN AND SAUSAGE HOTPOT   [M]

This recipe was inspired by the many hot sausage dishes served in Germany. However it is much simpler and quicker to make.

1 pint/600 ml chicken stock
2 lb/1 kg runner beans, stringed and cut into short lengths
4 oz/100 g streaky bacon
2 onions, chopped
½ teaspoon dried savory
1½ oz/40 g plain flour
salt and pepper
8 oz/225 g cooked sausages (English or German), sliced

Place the stock and beans in a pan and bring to the boil. Cover and simmer for 10 minutes. Meanwhile fry the bacon in a non-stick pan and add the onions when the fat begins to run. Fry gently for 5—6 minutes until the onions are tender. Stir in the savory, flour and seasoning.

Drain the liquid from the beans and gradually add it to the onion and bacon mixture, stirring all the time. Return to the boil and correct the seasoning.

Add the beans and sausage slices and cook for 5 minutes before serving with creamed potatoes.

BEANS WITH TOMATOES [A]

Runner beans are rarely found in the South of France but some friends of mine very successfully grow two rows every year. Here's the way they cook them with the sweet bell or plum tomatoes available there.

1 lb/450 g runner beans, topped and tailed
1 large onion, finely chopped
2 tablespoons olive oil
½ teaspoon allspice
salt and pepper
3 tomatoes, peeled and chopped
¼ pint/150 ml water
2 tablespoons dry sherry
pinch sugar

String the beans and cut into coarse chunks. Gently fry the onion in the olive oil until transparent. Add the beans, allspice and seasonings. Continue cooking gently for 5 minutes.

Add all the remaining ingredients and bring to the boil. Simmer uncovered for about 30 minutes until the beans are tender and the juices are fairly thick.

RUNNER BEANS WITH CORIANDER CREAM [A]

Coriander treated in this way has a quite different flavour to bought ground coriander.

1 tablespoon whole coriander seeds
4 tablespoons double cream
1 lb/450 g runner beans, topped, tailed and stringed
salt and pepper

Toast the whole coriander seeds under a hot grill until they begin to darken in colour. Coarsely crush with a rolling pin, or pound in a mortar, then sieve, discarding the large pieces. Mix the fine grains with the cream and keep on one side.

Cut the beans into lengths and cook in a steamer or in a very little lightly salted water until tender. Drain well.

Pour the coriander cream into a saucepan and bring to the boil. Cook for a minute or so and add the beans. Toss the sauce and season to taste. Serve at once.

INDIAN-STYLE BEANS WITH MUSTARD   [A]

Vary the amount of chilli in the recipe to give the required degree of heat to the dish.

1 lb/450 g runner beans
3 tablespoons cooking oil
1 teaspoon whole mustard seeds
2 cloves garlic, peeled and crushed
½ in/1 cm piece of root ginger, peeled and grated
1 small onion, finely chopped
½ dried red chilli, seeds removed, chopped
salt and freshly ground black pepper
½ teaspoon sugar

Top, tail and string the beans and cut into lengths. Blanch in boiling water for 3—4 minutes and then drain, and plunge into cold water.

Heat the cooking oil in a pan and dry the mustard seeds until they begin to pop. Add the garlic, ginger, onion and chilli and fry for 2—3 minutes until lightly browned. Add the beans, seasoning and sugar and turn down the heat. Cook gently, stirring from time to time, for 10—12 minutes.

BROCCOLI AND CALABRESE

Broccoli originated in Italy and has a long history. The Romans liked it and Tiberius's son Drusus is said to have eaten so much of it on one occasion that his father chided him for his greed. (Considering the general eating habits of the Roman aristocracy, though, it is difficult to believe that Drusus could have eaten so much that it would cause comment!) Broccoli came to the UK from the Continent in Elizabethan times and as a luxury item it was always treated with some care. A Stuart recipe suggests poaching it in milk and mace.

Various types of broccoli are now grown: calabrese — which is green sprouting broccoli, purple and white sprouting broccoli, and there is also Cape broccoli which looks more like a colourful cauliflower.

Availability: All the year round except calabrese which is only available from July to November.

Buying Guide: Look for a good colour with no yellowing of the leaves or flower heads. Stalks should snap easily.

Storage: Eat as soon as possible after purchase. Keep in a cool place until required.

Preparation: Cut off any tough looking stalks from calabrese. Wash and divide into sprigs. Wash and pick over sprouting broccoli. Chop for salads.

Basic Cooking: Cook calabrese and large broccoli in boiling salted water for 15—20 minutes. Take care not to overcook. The heads may remain firmer if they are steamed clear of the water. Cook other forms of sprouting broccoli in a little boiling salted water for 10—15 minutes. Serve with butter or a white or cheese sauce. Spears of calabrese are also very good served with hollandaise sauce.

BROCCOLI ECLAIRS [S]

Look out for the new ready-made choux pastry eclairs for a quick and speedy supper dish.

8 choux pastry eclairs
10 oz/300 g thick broccoli heads or calabrese
salt
1 oz/25 g butter
1 oz/25 g flour
½ pint/300 ml milk
pinch curry powder
2 oz/50 g Gruyère or Emmenthal cheese, grated
black pepper

Warm the choux buns in a low oven. Cook the broccoli heads in salted boiling water for 10 minutes. Remove with a slotted spoon, and cut off the stalks near to the heads. Return the stalks to the pan and cook for a further 10 minutes. Rub stalks through a sieve.

Melt the butter in a saucepan and stir in the flour. Add the milk and bring to the boil, whisking all the time with a wire whisk. Stir in the remaining ingredients and the stalk purée, and season to taste.

Slit the eclairs with a sharp knife. Spoon a good layer of sauce into the base of each eclair. Arrange the broccoli heads along the length of the eclairs and drizzle with remaining sauce.

BROCCOLI SALAD   [S]

The broccoli for this recipe only needs to be cooked for a very short time. If you overcook it, the broccoli will be too soft to make a good salad.

450 g/1 lb large broccoli heads
salt
1 hard-boiled egg, chopped
1 tomato, peeled, seeded and chopped
1 small sweet-sour pickled cucumber, finely chopped
4 spring onions, finely chopped
6 tablespoons salad oil
2 tablespoons cider vinegar
freshly ground black pepper
¼ teaspoon dried tarragon
pinch sugar

Steam the broccoli very briefly in a steamer or cook in a very little salted boiling water. Drain and leave to cool.

Mix the chopped egg, tomato, cucumber and spring onion in a small basin. Chill in the fridge. Mix the salad oil with the remaining ingredients and beat to an emulsion.

Arrange pieces of broccoli on four small serving plates and top with a little of the egg and cucumber mixture. Pour the dressing over the top and serve.

BROCCOLI AND MUSHROOM ROULADE   [M]

This is a really effective dish to serve at a dinner party. It is guaranteed to impress everyone.

4 oz/100 g button mushrooms, finely chopped
1 tablespoon cooking oil
4 eggs, separated
3 oz/75 g Cheddar cheese
1 teaspoon milk mustard
1 teaspoon plain flour
salt and pepper
1 lb/450 g broccoli
pinch grated nutmeg

Gently fry the mushrooms in the cooking oil for 2—3 minutes. Leave to cool. Beat the egg yolks with half the cheese, the mustard, the flour and the seasonings. Stir in the mushrooms.

Whisk the egg whites until stiff and then fold into the mushroom mixture. Spoon the mixture in a 12 x 9 in (30 x 22.5 cm) Swiss roll tin which has been lined with greased greaseproof paper. Bake at 200°C/400°F/Gas 6 for about 20 minutes until set throughout.

Meanwhile cook the broccoli in a little lightly salted boiling water or steam in a steamer. Drain well and purée or sieve. Mix with the remaining cheese and the nutmeg. Remove the roulade from the oven and quickly cover with the broccoli mixture. Starting with the shorter end gently roll up the roulade, removing the greaseproof paper as you go. Transfer to a heatproof plate and place in the oven for a further 2 minutes before serving.

BROCCOLI PASTA [M]

This unusual combination of flavours comes from an Italian friend who in turn received the recipe from her grandmother. Serve as a supper dish or in smaller quantities as a starter.

12 oz/350 g pasta shapes
1½ lb/700 g fresh broccoli spears, cut into pieces
5 tablespoons olive oil
1 oz/25 g butter
4 oz/100 g fresh breadcrumbs, wholemeal or white
1 small can anchovies, drained, washed and chopped
2 cloves garlic, peeled
1 green chilli pepper (optional)
freshly ground black pepper

Plunge the pasta and broccoli into boiling salted water and cook for about 10—12 minutes until both pasta and broccoli are just tender to the bite (*al dente*).

Meanwhile heat 3 tablespoons of the olive oil and the butter in a frying pan. Add the breadcrumbs and 2 anchovy fillets, and cook until the breadcrumbs are golden. In another pan heat the remaining oil and fry the whole cloves of garlic, the green chilli if used, and the remaining anchovy fillets.

Drain the pasta and broccoli well and pour the oil from the second pan through a sieve onto the pasta and broccoli. Toss well and put into a serving dish or arrange on four individual plates. Top with the fried breadcrumbs. Season with black pepper and serve at once.

CURRIED BROCCOLI WITH POTATOES   [A]

Use up leftover boiled potatoes and purple sprouting broccoli or calabrese in this Indian inspired dish.

3 tablespoons cooking oil
seeds from 2 cardamom pods
4 black peppercorns
1 clove
1 clove garlic, peeled and crushed
1 lb/450 g purple sprouting broccoli, thick stalks removed
8 oz/225 g cold cooked potatoes, diced
1 tablespoon plain yogurt
1 tablespoon ground cumin
1 teaspoon ground coriander
1 teaspoon curry powder
salt and black pepper

Heat the oil in a pan and fry the whole spices and the garlic for a minute or so. Add the broccoli and continue to fry gently, stirring from time to time, for about 6–8 minutes.

Stir in all the remaining ingredients and continue to cook over a low heat, stirring occasionally until the broccoli is tender and the potatoes are hot.

STIR-FRIED BROCCOLI WITH ALMONDS   [A]

Broccoli and calbrese take very well to the Chinese method of stir-frying. They retain both their bite and flavour.

2 oz/50 g flaked almonds
1 tablespoon cooking oil
1 onion, thinly sliced
1 lb/450 g purple sprouting broccoli, washed and cut into lengths
1 tablespoon soy sauce
pinch five-spice powder

Toast the flaked almonds in a dry frying pan to brown them. Remove from the pan and keep on one side.

Add the cooking oil to the pan and stir-fry the onion for 1 minute. Add the broccoli and continue stir-frying for a further 2 minutes. Add the soy sauce and five-spice powder and cook for a further minute. The broccoli should still be quite crunchy. Sprinkle with toasted almonds and serve at once.

SEPTEMBER

'The French fried potato has become an inescapable horror in almost every public eating place in the country. "French fries", say the menus, but they are not French fries any longer. They are a furry textured substance with the taste of plastic board.'

Russell Baker, 'Observer',
The New York Times,
February 22, 1968

Courgettes
Maincrop Potatoes
Sweetcorn
Vegetable Marrows

COURGETTES

Courgettes are baby marrows and are increasingly grown in place of the large vegetable marrow. They have always been popular in France and Italy where they are known as zucchini (in America as well). They are comparative newcomers to the UK, being first grown in Britain less than thirty years ago.

Availability: All the year round. They are cheapest from June to October.

Buying Guide: Choose smaller vegetables for cooking whole and the cheaper, larger ones for soups and made-up dishes. All courgettes should be firm to the touch and free from blemishes. There are also a few small round courgettes on sale. These taste much the same as the long ones.

Storage: Keep for two to three days in the salad compartment of the fridge.

Preparation: Wash and cut off each end. Cook whole, halved, sliced or diced. Slice for salads. Do not peel.

Basic Cooking: Steam or boil small courgettes in a very little salted boiling water. Toss in butter and serve with parsley or tarragon. Fry or grill halved or sliced vegetables and bake whole ones in foil or stuffed. Use also in soups and casseroles or stew with other vegetables such as onions, tomatoes and peppers. They are a vital ingredient of Ratatouille. Serve cold cooked courgettes with vinaigrette.

MARINATED COURGETTES [S]

This French provincial dish can be kept for a day or two in the fridge.

2 large courgettes (about 12oz/350 g)
4 tablespoons olive oil
salt and freshly ground black pepper
1 clove garlic, peeled and chopped

1 tablespoon chopped fresh sage leaves or 1 teaspoon dried
1 tablespoon red wine vinegar
¼ pint/150 ml dry white wine

Top and tail the courgettes and cut into thick slanting slices. Heat 2 tablespoons of the olive oil in a frying pan and lightly brown all slices of courgette on each side. Pack into a pâté dish, seasoning each layer as you go.

Pour the remaining oil into the frying pan and fry the garlic and sage until the garlic is brown. Add the vinegar and wine and bring to the boil. Pour over the courgettes so that the courgettes are fully covered.

Cover with foil and place in the fridge when cold. Leave for at least an hour before serving.

VENETIAN-STYLE COURGETTES   [S]

This unusual Italian dish makes a very good starter, or it can be served as a light supper dish. Increase the quantities in the latter case.

1 lb/450 g courgettes
1 oz/25 g butter
1 tablespoon olive oil
1 egg
1 oz/25 g Parmesan cheese, freshly grated
1 tablespoon double cream
1 tablespoon freshly chopped parsley or ½ teaspoon dried thyme
salt and black pepper

Trim the courgettes and slice lengthways. Cut each slice into two or three thick sticks. Heat the butter and oil in a frying pan and gently fry the courgettes over a low to medium heat for about 5 minutes. Do not allow the vegetables to brown.

Mix all the remaining ingredients, beat well with a fork and pour into the pan. Stir everything with a wooden spoon and, as soon as the egg sets, serve the dish with wholemeal rolls.

CASSEROLED COURGETTES WITH DILL [A]

Dill is a good flavouring to use with any kind of marrow or squash.

1 large onion, sliced
1 oz/25 g butter
1 lb/450 g courgettes, sliced
½ teaspoon dried dill leaves
salt and black pepper

Toss the onion and butter together over a low heat for about a minute. Add all the remaining ingredients and continue cooking gently for a further minute or two.

Transfer to a casserole and cover with a lid. Bake at 180°C/350°F/Gas 4 for about 45 minutes until the courgettes are just tender.

BAKED COURGETTE MOULDS WITH HERBS [A]

Serve these delicately flavoured vegetable moulds with plainly grilled meats or add a light tomato sauce and serve as a starter or light supper dish.

1 onion, finely chopped
1 clove garlic, crushed
2 tablespoons olive oil
1 lb/450 g courgettes, diced
1 oz/25 g white bread, without crusts
3 fl.oz/75 ml milk
1 tablespoon freshly chopped mint
salt and black pepper
2 eggs, beaten

Fry the onion and garlic in olive oil for a minute or two until onion turns transparent. Add the courgettes and continue frying over a gentle heat for about 15 minutes, stirring from time to time.

Mix the bread and milk with the herbs and seasoning and leave to stand. When the courgettes are cooked, mash the bread and milk well with a fork. Stir in the eggs and then the courgette mixture.

Spoon into individual moulds or one large mould and place in a baking tin filled with 2 in/5 cm hot water. Bake at 180°C/350°F/Gas 4 for 50–60 minutes until set through the centre.

COURGETTES SOUTHERN-STYLE   [A]

Try using either fresh coriander leaves or ground coriander seeds in this spicy recipe which comes from the southern states of America.

4 tablespoons cooking oil
1 lb/450 g courgettes, thickly sliced
1 x 14 oz/400 g can tomatoes
4 tablespoons tomato purée
1 fresh green chilli, seeded and finely chopped
1 clove garlic, crushed
4 sprigs fresh coriander, chopped, or ½ teaspoon ground coriander
$\frac{1}{8}$ teaspoon dried rosemary
salt and pepper
3 oz/75 g Cheddar cheese, grated

Heat the oil in a frying pan and fry the courgettes on each side until lightly browned. Drain on kitchen paper.

Place the contents of the can of tomatoes, the tomato purée, chopped chilli, garlic, coriander, rosemary and seasoning in a saucepan. Bring to the boil and cook for 5 minutes.

Arrange the courgettes in a shallow ovenproof dish and pour the tomato mixture over the top. Sprinkle with grated cheese and bake at 200°C/400°F/Gas 6 for 30 minutes.

MAINCROP POTATOES

The potato, discovered in the New World by the Conquistadores, was first taken to Spain — but no one wanted to eat them, though they were grown in botanical gardens. The Spanish objected to potatoes on various grounds, ranging from the fear that they caused leprosy to a belief that they caused excessive flatulence! After limited acceptance in Spain, potato cultivation spread to Italy and Germany and then to Ireland.

The Irish were the first to plant and consume potatoes on a large scale and by the end of the seventeenth century potatoes were the most important food crop in Ireland. It was a good two hundred years before England and Scotland started to cultivate potatoes on anything like the Irish scale, and France — the home of *pommes frites* or chips — was the last to adopt potatoes into its national cuisine.

Potatoes also moved to North America, but rather surprisingly via Europe rather than direct from their native South America. They were introduced by Scottish-Irish immigrants in the early eighteenth century.

On the medicinal front, the carrying of a hard black potato was thought, in seventeenth- to eighteenth-century Britain, to help rheumatism, and the juice was rubbed into arthritic joints to help relieve the pain (a remedy used by schoolchildren before a caning).

Potato dishes of all kinds abound in European and transatlantic cuisine. They include Boxty, Bubble and Squeak, Pommes Anna, Gnocchi di Patate, Rösti and Kartoffelküchen among many others.

Maincrop is the name given by the trade to 'old' potatoes. The uses to which potatoes can be put is almost endless!

Availability: September to June.

Buying Guide: Avoid potatoes with green or black patches, mechanical damage or growth shoots. Buy in bulk for convenience and economy.

Storage: If buying in bulk empty the sack completely and use any which show signs of damage at once. If the rest are dry and reasonably clean return to the sack and keep in a cool, dry frost-free place, preferably raised from the ground. Keep in the dark. When storing weekly purchases remove from polythene bags and store in dark, dry and airy conditions.

Preparation: The best maincrop potatoes may be cooked in their skin. Others may need to be peeled as thinly as possible.

Basic Cooking: Cook in lightly salted boiling water, bake, roast, fry or sauté. Use in soups and stews and as toppings for savoury dishes. Add potato to counteract over-salted casseroles.

HAWAIIAN NESTS　　　　　　　　　　　　　　　　　　[M]

Piped potatoes are delicious filled with a savoury sauce and they make an excellent supper dish served with peas or beans or a green salad. Allow two nests per person.

1¾ lb/800 g potatoes, washed
knob of butter
2 eggs, beaten
salt and pepper

Filling
½ oz/15 g butter
½ oz/15 g flour
¼ pint/150 ml milk
salt and pepper
6 oz/175 g cooked ham, chopped
2 rings canned pineapple, chopped
parsley to garnish

Cook the potatoes in lightly salted boiling water for about 15–20 minutes until tender. Drain, peel if necessary, and mash with butter. Stir in the remaining ingredients. Pipe nest shapes on a greased baking tray and bake at 200°C/400°F/Gas 6 for 15 minutes until lightly browned.

Meanwhile, melt the butter in a saucepan, stir in the flour and gradually add the milk, stirring all the time. Bring to the boil, add the seasoning, and cook for 2–3 minutes. Add the ham and most of the pineapple.

Transfer the cooked nests to a serving plate and fill with the ham and pineapple mixture. Top each nest with a piece of retained pineapple, garnish with sprigs of parsley, and serve.

PARSLEY POTATO MOUNTAINS   [A]

Serve this tasty variation on duchesse potatoes with both casseroles and roasts, or with baked fish.

1¾ lb/800 g potatoes, washed
knob of butter
2 eggs, beaten
4 tablespoons freshly chopped parsley
salt and pepper

Cook the potatoes until tender. Drain, peel if necessary, and mash with butter. Stir in the remaining ingredients. The mixture should be fairly soft.

Spoon into mounds on a greased baking tray. Bake at 200°C/400°F/Gas 6 for 15 minutes until lightly browned.

POTATO KIDSON [A]

A friend produced this delicious potato dish to go with fried liver, but it is also good with any kind of grilled or fried meat.

1½ lb/700 g potatoes, peeled and chopped
salt
1 apple, peeled, cored and chopped
juice of ½ lemon
2 rashers streaky bacon, diced
1 onion, finely chopped
butter
2 oz/50 g button mushrooms, finely chopped

Cook the potatoes in boiling salted water until tender. About 5 minutes before the end of the cooking time add the apple (which has been coated with the lemon juice). Drain well and mash together.

Meanwhile fry the bacon in a non-stick pan and when the fat starts to run add the onion and a little butter if necessary. When the onion has softened, add the mushrooms and fry gently for a further 3—4 minutes until tender.

Mix the fried vegetables into the mashed potatoes. Reheat, if necessary, over a low heat and serve.

JACKET-BAKED POTATOES WITH CORIANDER [A]

These deliciously spicy potatoes go particularly well with plainly grilled lamb chops.

4 large potatoes
1—2 teaspoons ground coriander, to taste
1 oz/25 g butter
salt and pepper

Scrub the potatoes and bake in their jackets until tender (a good hour at 190—200°C/375—400°F/Gas 5—6). Toast the coriander in a small dry frying pan and keep on one side.

When the potatoes are cooked cut off the tops and scoop out the flesh from the main body of the potato. Mash the potato flesh with the toasted coriander, butter and seasonings and pile back into the potato. Replace the top and bake for a further 5—10 minutes.

SPICED POTATOES [A]

These delicately spiced potatoes are good served with plainly grilled meats and roasts. They can also be served with Indian food.

1 tablespoon cooking oil
1 teaspoon whole cumin seeds
½ teaspoon curry powder
¼ teaspoon ground bay leaves
¼ teaspoon celery salt
freshly ground black pepper
1½ lb /700 g potatoes, peeled and cubed
5 oz/150 g plain yogurt

Heat the cooking oil in a good-sized pan and fry the cumin seeds for about a minute. Add the rest of the herbs and spices and fry for a little longer. Next add the potatoes and stir to make sure that they are well coated with the spices. Pour on the yogurt, stir, and bring to the boil.

Cover and simmer for 20–30 minutes, stirring occasionally, until the potatoes are tender and most of the liquid has been absorbed.

SPICED POTATOES WITH CAULIFLOWER [A]

As a variation on the above, add florets of par-boiled cauliflower to the potatoes after they have been cooking for 15 minutes.

POTATO CAKE [A]

Serve with butter as an alternative to bread with a main course salad or with boiled or scrambled eggs.

2 lb/1 kg potatoes, peeled and quartered
salt
1 oz/25 g butter
black pepper
4 oz/100 g plain flour

Cook the potatoes in lightly salted boiling water for about 15 minutes until just tender. Drain and dry over a low heat. Mash with butter and seasonings. Stir in the flour.

Shape into an oval, about ¼ in/6 mm thick, on a greased baking tray. Mark into squares with a knife. Bake at 190°C/375°F/Gas 5 for 40—45 minutes until well browned and crisp at the edges. Break into squares to serve.

SWEETCORN

Sweetcorn or corn on the cob is a type of maize which was originally cultivated by North and South American Indians. Columbus ate corn during his travels in Peru, and it was the Spaniards who brought maize seed to Europe in the sixteenth century. Until recent years in the UK it was only considered fit for animals but it has been popular in the US for many years. It may have been the American forces stationed in the UK during the 1939—1945 war who were responsible for the change in attitude here. It is sometimes known as Indian corn but this is actually a coarser variety.

Availability: July to October.

Buying Guide: Always examine the corn itself, if necessary gently pulling away the green sheath. The corn should be full, round and plump with a bright creamy colour. The corn should not be at all wizened and the silk tassel at the end of the cob should not be black and dead.

Storage: Eat as soon as possible after purchase. Keep in a cool place until needed.

Preparation: Trim off the tassel, outer leaves and stalks. For some recipes the corn kernels may need to be removed from the cob before cooking. To do this, use a sharp knife and, holding the stalk end upwards, make downward strokes with the knife, turning the cob after each slice until all the corn has been cut away.

Basic Cooking: Plunge the washed cob into boiling water for about 10 minutes. It may take longer to cook if it is older. But over-cooking makes the corn tough. Add sugar but no salt to the cooking liquor. Alternatively brush with butter or wrap in foil, and bake in the oven. Use the kernels in casseroles and made dishes and cooked kernels in salads.

CORN AND PRAWN PUDDING [M]

This is an American recipe from Iowa.

3 corn on the cob
2 oz/50 g Ritz biscuits, crumbled
1 egg, beaten
¼ pint/150 ml milk
4 oz/100 g peeled prawns
½ green pepper, seeded and finely chopped
1 onion, grated
½ teaspoon Worcestershire sauce
2 oz/50 g Cheddar cheese, grated

Cut the corn from the cob with a sharp knife.

Mix together all the ingredients except the cheese and spoon into a greased casserole dish. Bake at 180°C/350°F/Gas 4 for 50 minutes until set in the centre. Sprinkle with the cheese and bake for a further 8—10 minutes.

SWEETCORN AND EGG VOL-AU-VENTS [M]

The scrambled egg base to this recipe makes an unusual filling for vol-au-vent cases. It can also be used to fill large blind-baked pastry cases.

2 large corn on the cob
salt
5 tablespoons milk
large knob of butter
5 eggs, beaten
1 teaspoon dried tarragon
black pepper
8 vol-au-vent cases

Cut the corn from the cob and cook in lightly salted boiling water for about 6 minutes, taking care not to overcook the corn.

Meanwhile heat the milk and butter in a pan. Add the beaten eggs and cook over a moderate heat, stirring with a fork all the time. When the eggs are lightly scrambled remove the eggs from the heat and stir in the tarragon and the well drained sweetcorn, and season to taste.

Use this mixture to fill the vol-au-vent cases. Place in a hot oven at 200°C/400°F/Gas 6 for 4—5 minutes.

AMERICAN CURRIED CORN [A]

This recipe was given to me by a friend in Carolina where they sometimes use a spoonful of peanut butter in place of the curry powder.

1 oz/25 g butter
1 clove garlic, finely chopped
1 onion, finely chopped
4 corn on the cob
1 tablespoon curry powder
salt and pepper
¼ pint/150 ml soured cream or yogurt
2—3 green chillies, seeded and chopped

Melt the butter and fry the garlic and onion for 3—4 minutes until lightly browned.

Cut the corn from the cobs with a sharp knife and add to the pan. Stir and add all the remaining ingredients. Bring to the boil, reduce the heat and simmer gently for 20 minutes.

CORN FRITTERS [A]

Serve these crunchy fritters with Chicken Maryland or indeed any kind of chicken dish.

2 eggs
2½ fl. oz/75 ml milk
½ tablespoon melted butter
3 oz/75 g plain flour
½ teaspoon baking powder
salt
4 small corn on the cob
cooking oil

Beat the eggs, milk and butter together. Sift the flour, baking powder and salt into a bowl. Make a well in the centre and pour in the egg mixture. Beat to a smooth batter.

Cut the corn from the cob and stir into the batter.

Heat the cooking oil in a deep-fat fryer and drop tablespoonfuls of the corn mixture into the hot fat. Fry for 2—3 minutes until golden. Drain on kitchen paper and serve at once.

CORN AND HAM FRITTERS   [A]

Use two corn on the cob instead of four, and add 4 oz/100 g diced cooked ham and 2 oz/50 g of cooked peas to the batter mixture, and continue as above. Serve with freshly made tomato sauce (page 46), or make much smaller fritters and serve as cocktail canapés.

VEGETABLE MARROWS

The larger versions of the popular courgette may be light or dark green or yellow in colour. They can be an extremely economical buy, for one large marrow may make a vegetable dish for two *plus* a soup, or it can serve as the basis for a main course for more.

The origins of the vegetable marrow are obscure although it is probably native to Central America. How and when it first reached the UK is unknown. Some experts think it may have come via the Middle East. However, by 1882, vegetable marrows were extremely popular. The Victorians liked nothing better than to compete in the growing of larger and larger varieties.

Availability: April to October, peaking in August and September.

Buying Guide: The best size for a vegetable marrow is about 12 in/ 30 cm in length. Choose one with a tender skin which has a full shine to it. Use larger marrows for soup or chutney.

Storage: Store in a cool, dry, airy place and eat within a day or two.

Preparation: Peel and remove the seeds. Cut in half, lengthways, and stuff or cut into cubes.

Basic Cooking: Steam in a steamer or in a very little salted boiling water. Serve sprinkled with paprika pepper or serve with a cream, cheese or tomato sauce. Alternatively gently fry and serve with sautéed onion and tomato with thyme or marjoram or bake in the oven.

MARROW WITH MACARONI   [S]

Marrow makes a really juicy accompaniment to macaroni which can sometimes be rather dry.

1 onion, thinly sliced
2 tablespoons olive oil
knob of butter
1 small vegetable marrow, peeled, seeded and diced
1 tablespoon freshly chopped basil
1 tablespoon tomato purée
salt and pepper
6 oz/175 g quick-cook short macaroni

Fry the onion in 1 tablespoon of the olive oil and the butter until very lightly browned. Add the marrow dice to the pan. Continue cooking over a low heat, stirring from time to time until the marrow just begins to soften. This will take about 8 minutes depending on the size of the dice. Stir in the basil and tomato purée and season to taste.

Meanwhile cook the macaroni as directed on the packet. Drain very well and then sauté in the remaining oil. Add the marrow mixture and toss well together. Serve sprinkled with freshly ground black pepper.

FRIED MARROW WITH BACON ROLLS [M]

This very unusual treatment for vegetable marrow was inspired by an idea in a household encyclopedia from the 1930s.

12 rashers streaky bacon
1 small marrow
2–3 tablespoons plain flour
salt and pepper
1 egg, beaten
3 oz/75 g dried breadcrumbs
cooking oil

Cut the rashers into two pieces and roll up. Place under the grill and cook until crisp.

Peel the marrow and cut into slices. Cut out the seeds. Mix the flour and seasonings and use to dust the marrow rings. Dip the rings in beaten egg and then in breadcrumbs, making sure they are well coated.

Shallow-fry for about 10 minutes on each side or deep-fry in hot cooking oil for about 3–4 minutes until golden in colour. Serve with bacon rolls in the centre of each slice.

HUNGARIAN-STYLE MARROW   [A]

One of my favourite Hungarian restaurants in London serves marrow this way and after some persuading the chef finally consented to part with the recipe.

1 medium vegetable marrow
1 small onion, sliced and fried in a little butter
2 tablespoons fresh chopped dill or 1 tablespoon dried
1 tablespoon vegetable stock or water
6 tablespoons double cream

Peel the marrow and then cut in half and remove the seeds. Cut into small cubes. Mix with the fried onion and dill and place in a casserole dish with a very little water or stock. Cover and bake at 190°C/375°F/Gas 5 for 45 minutes.

Drain off the cooking liquor and mix it with the cream. Pour into a saucepan and bring to the boil. Continue boiling for 3—4 minutes. When the mixture thickens pour over the marrow and serve.

MARROW WITH SWEET-SOUR CUCUMBER SAUCE   [A]

Add 2 cubed sweet-sour cucumbers to the above recipe and continue as before. This gives the dish an extra tang.

OCTOBER

'A tale twice told is a cabbage twice sold.'

Traditional proverb

Celeriac
Cabbage
Onions
Beansprouts

CELERIAC

Celeriac was developed from celery from which it gets its name. It is actually a type of celery which has been grown for its root rather than its stem. It is a large rather lumpy root with a flavour somewhat like celery but with a hint of parsnip or fennel.

It is very popular in France, Italy and Germany where it is grown and cooked in large quantities. Almost every delicatessen in France sells a salad of blanched sticks of celeriac in a mustard-flavoured mayonnaise.

Availability: September to April.

Buying Guide: Look for firm roots and avoid any which show signs of rotting or are badly damaged. Avoid really large specimens.

Storage: Keep in a cool, airy place for a week or so until required.

Preparation: Wash and slice and then peel. Grate for salads or cut into sticks or dice to cook.

Basic Cooking: Boil in salted water for about 30 minutes depending on the size of the pieces. Toss in butter or serve in a good white or cheese sauce. Purée with milk and butter or other vegetables. Alternatively par-boil and fry on its own or with other vegetables. Serve cold with mayonnaise or *rémoulade* sauce.

WHITING WITH CELERIAC [M]

The rather bland flavour of the whiting allows the flavour from the vegetables to permeate the fish.

1½ lb/700 g carrots, peeled and cut into thin sticks
3 oz/75 g butter
1½ lb/700 g celeriac, peeled and cut into thin sticks
4 oz/100 g button mushrooms, cut into sticks
salt and pepper
1 teaspoon freshly chopped tarragon or ½ teaspoon dried
4 fillets of whiting, skinned
4 tablespoons dry vermouth
4 tablespoons double cream (optional)

Gently sauté the carrots in a pan with the butter. After 5 minutes add the celeriac, and after a further 5 minutes the mushrooms. Continue cooking very gently for a further 10 minutes, stirring from time to time. Stir in the seasoning and tarragon.

Place this mixture in the base of a shallow heatproof dish and arrange the whiting fillets on the top. Moisten all over with the dry vermouth and season the fish. Cover with foil and bake at 180°C/350°F/Gas 4 for about 25–30 minutes until the fish is cooked. Serve at once.

For a richer effect carefully pour the juices into a saucepan and add the cream. Bring to the boil and cook for 2–3 minutes until the sauce thickens a little. Pour over the fish and serve.

CELERIAC AND CARROT FLAN [M]

Almost any root vegetable can be treated in this way. The vegetables remain just slightly crunchy. Serve the flan as part of a hot buffet or as a supper dish.

6 oz/175 g shortcrust pastry
6 oz/175 g celeriac, peeled and finely grated
2 oz/50 g carrots, peeled and finely grated
3 oz/75 g Cheddar cheese, grated
2 eggs
4 tablespoons milk
salt and pepper

Roll out the pastry and use to line a 7 in/17.5 cm shallow flan tin. Mix the grated vegetables and the grated cheese. Stir in the egg, milk and seasoning and spoon into the pastry case.

Bake at 200°C/400°F/Gas 6 for about an hour until the flan is set in the centre and lightly browned.

CELERIAC AND TOMATO CASSEROLE [A]

Serve this dish with grilled chicken or with an omelette.

1 onion, sliced
1 tablespoon cooking oil
1 medium-sized celeriac, peeled and diced
1 x 14 oz/500 g can tomatoes
¼ teaspoon grated lemon rind

juice of ½ lemon
pinch mixed herbs
salt and freshly ground black pepper

Gently fry the onion in cooking oil for about 3—4 minutes until transparent. Add the celeriac and continue to fry gently for a further 2—3 minutes. Add all the remaining ingredients and bring to the boil.

Simmer for 40 minutes until the celeriac is tender and the sauce is fairly thick.

CELERIAC WITH SESAME SEEDS   [A]

This recipe was inspired by an Indian recipe using potatoes, but celeriac works equally well. Parsnips, swedes or yams could also be used or a mixture of two of them such as potatoes and swedes or yams and parsnips.

4 tablespoons cooking oil
3 teaspoons whole sesame seeds
2 teaspoons whole cumin seeds
1 teaspoon whole black mustard seeds
1½ lb/700 g cold cooked celeriac, diced
salt and cayenne pepper
1 tablespoon lemon juice

Heat the cooking oil until fairly hot. Add the seeds and fry for half a minute or so until they begin to pop. Add the celeriac, seasonings and lemon juice and continue cooking for a further 5 minutes.

SPECIAL TIP: Purée celeriac in the way described on page 14, or, for a special dinner, use instead of mushrooms in French Mushrooms Flans (page 30).

CABBAGE

Cabbage must be one of the most under-rated and over-exposed vegetables in the British culinary repertoire. All too often it appears as a sort of pale green, soggy mass, contributing little to the flavour of the meat though rather more to the smell in the kitchen.

Perhaps it is not so surprising that this vegetable is so consistently overcooked for it always has been. The Celt, the Roman, the Anglo-Saxon peasant and the Elizabethan chef all felt that the only possible treatment was to add it to a broth and boil it to death or to cook it equally well in plain water and then to purée it.

In other countries, notably Germany and other parts of Eastern Europe and Russia, it has fared rather better. The Germans have even found a way of preserving cabbage so that it retains all its natural goodness for quite a long time. The cabbage is fermented and mixed with various herbs and spices to form *sauerkraut*.

In other parts of the world cabbage is used in soups and in Pot au Feu, but the cabbage is not added until towards the end of the cooking time. It has also been stuffed, used in pies and layered with eggs and cheese to make a savoury cake.

There are quite a few different kinds of cabbage on the market at different times of the year. Choose from greens and spring cabbage, Savoy Cabbage, with its crinkly leaves, red cabbage, green cabbage and white cabbage.

Availability: One or more of the above types is available throughout the year.

Buying Guide: Green varieties should always have a good colour with no signs of yellowing. White cabbage should not be loose or have any brown smudges. Red cabbage should have a 'bloom' on the outside and be free from any dark brown patches. It should also be tightly solid.

Storage: Green cabbages and greens do not store well and should be used as soon as possible after purchase. Savoys, however, will keep for a week in a cool, dry, airy place. So will red and white cabbages.

Preparation: Wash well and remove any tough outer leaves. Shred the cabbage to eat raw and shred or quarter before cooking.

Basic Cooking: Boil or steam in a very little salted water until just tender. Chop again with butter and pepper. White and green cabbages may be flavoured with juniper berries, caraway seeds or dried thyme in the cooking water. Red cabbage goes well with cooking apples and vinegar. All cabbage may also be baked in the oven with sliced onions and other chosen flavourings. Cook in a casserole dish with a lid.

RUSSIAN CABBAGE PIE [M]

This pie can be topped with shortcrust pastry in place of potatoes.

½ teaspoon caraway seeds
4 cardamom pods
½ pint/300 ml soured cream
1 oz/25 g butter
2 lb/1 kg white cabbage, finely shredded
salt and black pepper
8 oz/225 g cooked ham or lean bacon, diced
4 hard-boiled eggs, sliced
1½ lb/700 g potatoes, peeled and cooked

Crush the caraway seeds and the cardamom seeds, discarding the pods. Mix with the soured cream and keep on one side.

Melt the butter in a large pan and add the cabbage. Fry gently for 3—4 minutes until the cabbage softens. Pour on the soured cream and add the seasoning. Cover with a lid and cook over a low heat for 40 minutes, stirring occasionally.

Mix the ham or bacon into the cabbage and transfer the mixture to a casserole or pie dish. Arrange a layer of sliced hard-boiled eggs over the top and add a little more seasoning. Mash the potatoes with a little butter and milk and spread over the dish, forking the top into an attractive pattern. Bake at 190°C/375°F/Gas 5 for 30 minutes.

BRAISED CABBAGE WITH GRAPEFRUIT [A]

The tangy flavour of the grapefruit makes cabbage taste quite different. Serve with any kind of roast meat and cook at the same time.

½ large green Savoy cabbage, shredded
2 Granny Smith apples, peeled, cored and chopped
juice of 1 grapefruit
10 oz/300 g plain yogurt
salt and pepper

Mix the cabbage and apple together and place in a casserole dish. Pour the grapefruit juice over the top, cover and bake at 200°C/400°F/Gas 6 for 45 minutes.

Stir in the yogurt and seasonings, cover again and continue cooking for a further 15 minutes.

WHITE CABBAGE AND FRUIT COLESLAW   [A]

This variation on the classic American Coleslaw uses fruit and nuts to make a much more interesting salad. Serve with cold meats or as part of a cold buffet.

½ a medium-sized white cabbage
2 tablespoons salad oil
2 teaspoons wine vinegar
salt
freshly ground black pepper
4 sticks celery
2 red apples
2 oz/50 g raisins
2 oz/50 g chopped walnuts
4 oz/100 g grapes, halved and seeded
1 tablespoon chopped chives

Finely shred the cabbage and put into a bowl. Mix together the oil, vinegar, salt and pepper and stir into the cabbage to moisten slightly.

Chop the celery into matchstick strips, and core and chop the red apples. Add them to the cabbage along with the raisins, walnuts, grapes and chives. Mix together and serve.

CABBAGE AND VEGETABLE CASSEROLE   [A]

Any kind of cabbage can be used for this substantial vegetable casserole. Turn into a main course by serving with plenty of grated cheese sprinkled over each portion.

1 lb/450 g cabbage, shredded
2 large onions, sliced
2 large leeks, sliced
2 oz/50 g butter
2 tablespoons freshly chopped mint or ½ teaspoon dried
salt and pepper

Layer the vegetables in a casserole dish adding a few knobs of butter and sprinkling mint and seasonings over each layer. Finish with a layer of cabbage. Cover with a lid and bake at 190°C/ 375°F/Gas 5 for about an hour until the vegetables are tender.

BRAISED RED CABBAGE [A]

The oranges and raisins in this recipe complement the cabbage well and give an unusual flavour to the finished dish. Serve with roast pork or veal.

½ oz/15 g butter
1 onion, sliced
1 lb/450 g red cabbage, finely shredded
1 oz/25 g raisins
grated rind of 1 orange
2 tablespoons redcurrant jelly
2 tablespoons cider vinegar

Melt the butter and fry the onions for about 4—5 minutes until softened and lightly browned. Add the cabbage and continue cooking and stirring occasionally for a further 10 minutes.

Mix the remaining ingredients and add to the pan. Stir well and bring to the boil. Cover and simmer for 30 minutes until the cabbage is tender and most of the liquid has been taken up.

BAKED RICE WITH WHITE CABBAGE [A]

This makes a very useful all-in-one vegetable and rice dish which can be cooked in the oven with almost any kind of casserole.

12 oz/350 g white cabbage, shredded
2 onions, sliced
6 oz/175 g long-grain rice
12 fl. oz/350 ml chicken stock
¼ teaspoon dried thyme
salt and black pepper

Mix the cabbage and onion together and layer with the rice in a casserole dish. Mix the chicken stock with the thyme and seasonings and pour over the rice and vegetables.

Cover with a lid and bake at 180°C/350°F/Gas 4 for 45—50 minutes until all the liquid has been absorbed and the rice is tender.

ONIONS

Onions are older than recorded history and in their time they have featured as a symbol of perfection, as the key to the gates of heaven, and as a very powerful medicine. The Egyptians carried their veneration of the onion so far that the priests forbade the eating of it, and bouquets of the plant were placed in the hands of important mummies to enable them to get into the afterworld. Even in Britain, onions were believed to be capable of frightening off all evil, and were often carried as a protection against witches and snakes.

Country people used to recommend the placing of a cut onion in a sick room to help drive off disease, and the idea seems not to have been all that misguided for modern research has shown that onion juice does seem to attract germs.

Onions also have a very long culinary history and they are still used to flavour many of our classic dishes. They are also very good served as a dish in their own right.

Availability: All the year round.

Buying Guide: Choose firm dry onions with feathery skins and avoid those which are soft and flabby or showing signs of sprouting. Look out, too, for the small pickling onions which may also be used as a casserole garnish, and the purple coloured shallots. The latter have a good flavour and are used in quite a lot of French recipes.

Storage: Store for a week or more in a cool, dry and airy place.

Preparation: Cut off each end and peel. Cook whole, sliced or chopped. Finely chop for salads.

Basic Cooking: Steam whole onions in a very little salted water. Serve with a white or a tomato sauce or push out the centres, stuff and bake in the oven. Braise whole onions in stock or wine with butter and other flavourings. Fry in butter or oil or deep-fry rings coated in batter. Bake in the oven and use in soups, casseroles, flans and all kinds of made dishes.

SAGE AND ONION TARTLETS   [S]

Sage and onion is a classic combination for sauces and stuffings and this same combination works equally well in these unusual tartlets. Serve as a starter or as part of a cocktail buffet.

8 oz/225 g shortcrust pastry
2 large onions, grated
2 oz/50 g butter
1 teaspoon dried sage
1 oz/25 g Cheddar cheese, finely grated
2 eggs, beaten
4 fl. oz/100 ml double cream
salt and pepper

Roll out the pastry and use to line twelve small tartlet tins.

Fry the onion in the butter until soft and transparent. Stir in the sage, cheese, eggs and cream and season.

Spoon this mixture into the tartlets and bake at 190°C/375°F/ Gas 5 for 30 minutes until the pastry is cooked and the tartlets are golden on top.

ITALIAN-STYLE LIVER WITH ONIONS   [M]

Ask the butcher to cut the liver into really thin slices.

1¼ lb/575 g onions, sliced
1 tablespoon cooking oil
½ oz/15 g butter
4 tablespoons dry sherry (or Martini)
½ teaspoon dried thyme or sage, or grated orange rind
salt and pepper
12 oz/350 g lamb's or calf's liver, thinly sliced

Gently fry the onions in oil and butter for 4—5 minutes until they turn transparent and begin to soften. Pour on the sherry (or Martini) and stir in the herbs and seasoning. Bring the mixture to the boil. Reduce the heat and simmer.

Lay the pieces of liver on top of the onions and cook for 5 minutes. Turn over and repeat on the second side. Remove the liver from the pan and keep warm. Turn up the heat to reduce any excess liquid. Spoon the onions over the liver and serve at once.

SCALLOPED ONIONS [A]

This traditional recipe also works well with a mixture of leeks and onions, or leeks alone.

1½ lb/700 g onions, sliced
1 oz/25 g butter
1 oz/25 g fresh wholemeal breadcrumbs
salt and pepper
½ oz/15 g Parmesan cheese, grated

Gently fry the onions in butter to soften them. Layer the fried onions in a casserole with the breadcrumbs and seasoning. End with a layer of breadcrumbs, sprinkle with Parmesan and bake at 190°C/375°F/Gas 5 for 30 minutes.

SPECIAL TIP. For an unusual accompaniment and garnish to grilled chicken or grilled pork chops, cut 4 small onions into rings and place in a pan with 2 tablespoons lemon juice and 1 teaspoon dried tarragon. Put on a very low heat, cover with a tight-fitting lid and leave for 15 minutes. Most of the liquid will have disappeared and the onions will have softened.

ONION AND FENNEL SAMBAL [A]

This piquant little salad goes very well with all kinds of Eastern food. It also works well with grilled meats and kebabs.

1 large onion, finely chopped
½ head fennel, finely chopped
¼ green pepper, finely chopped
2 tablespoons freshly chopped parsley
juice and rind of 1 lemon
pinch cayenne pepper or ground chilli
salt and black pepper

Mix all the ingredients just before serving and toss well together.

ONION BREAD [A]

This unusual bread comes from Syria. Try it warm with hard-boiled eggs, black olives and salad.

1 small onion, finely chopped
3 tablespoons olive oil
8 oz/225 g self-raising flour
½ teaspoon salt
1 teaspoon baking powder
½ teaspoon dried thyme
milk

Gently fry the onion in the olive oil until it turns transparent.

Sift the flour, salt and baking powder into a bowl. Add the thyme and mix well with a spoon. Make a well in the centre and add the fried onions and sufficient water to make a fairly soft dough. Turn out onto a floured surface and knead for about 10 minutes until the dough is elastic and no longer sticks to your hands. Place in a 1 lb/450 g loaf tin and leave in a warm place for about an hour to rise.

Brush the top with milk. Bake at 180°C/350°F/Gas 4 for about 80 to 85 minutes until golden on top and a skewer comes out clean. Remove from the tin and leave to cool on a wire rack.

BEANSPROUTS

Beansprouts have been known to the Chinese for thousands of years but they are relatively new to the West. They have a delicate flavour and a crunchy texture, but both these attributes are lost if they are overcooked.

Beansprouts are extremely nutritious. In addition to the original protein content of the bean, the vitamin content increases as the bean starts to sprout. Beansprouts also contain enzymes which help in the digestion process, and minerals in a form which is easily used by our bodies. Beansprouts are one of the freshest vegetables we have, since they are still growing when we eat them.

In addition to the better-known Chinese beansprouts — sprouted mung beans — there are sprouted alfalfa, lentils, soya beans and wheat, which are on sale increasingly in supermarkets and health food shops.

Beans can be sprouted at home.

Availability: All the year round.

Buying Guide: Look at the base of the pack to see that there is no liquid in it. Choose packs which look fresh and crisp.

Storage: Eat as soon as possible after purchase. Keep in the salad drawer of the fridge until needed.

Preparation: Use directly from the pack. There is no need to wash the beansprouts. Eat raw as they are.

Basic Cooking: Use in stir-fry recipes or add to soup and casseroles just before they are served. Any longer cooking will render them limp and tasteless.

BEANSPROUT AND CHEESE SALAD [M]

Any kind of beansprouts can be used in this recipe but it works particularly well with short stemmed soya bean or lentil sprouts.

6 oz/175 g beansprouts
4 sticks celery, finely sliced
6—8 radishes, chopped
2 large spring onions, finely chopped
1 box cress
6 oz/175 g Tilsit or Danbo cheese, cut into strips
juice of ½ lemon
black pepper

Place all the ingredients in a large bowl and toss well together. Serve at once.

DEVILLED BEANSPROUTS [A]

Use the long commercially grown Chinese or mung beansprouts for this recipe,·and serve with grilled lamb or pork chops or as part of an Eastern-style meal.

1 small onion, very finely chopped
1 stick celery, very finely chopped
1 tablespoon cooking oil
12 oz/350 g Chinese beansprouts
1 teaspoon Tewkesbury mustard
1 teaspoon Worcestershire sauce
4 tablespoons soured cream

salt and freshly ground black pepper
1 tablespoon freshly chopped parsley

Gently fry the onion and celery in cooking oil for about 5—6 minutes until fairly tender. Stir from time to time and do not allow the vegetables to brown. Add the beansprouts and stir-fry with the other vegetables for 2—3 minutes.

Mix all the remaining ingredients in a cup and pour into the pan. Bring to the boil. Toss the ingredients together and serve at once.

CHINESE BEANSPROUT SALAD   [A]

I encountered this dish in one of the authentic Chinese restaurants on the edge of Soho. It's very easy to make at home and delicious with any kind of Chinese meal. It also goes well with plain roast meats.

4 oz/100 g Chinese egg noodles
4—6 spring onions, sliced lengthways
6 oz/175 g Chinese beansprouts
2 oz/50 g carrots, coarsely shredded
½ green pepper, seeded and cut into sticks
2 tablespoons salad oil
1 tablespoon soy sauce
1—2 teaspoons lemon juice
½ teaspoon grated fresh root ginger
pinch five-spice powder

Cook the Chinese noodles as directed on the pack. Drain well and leave to cool. Chop coarsely if the noodles are very long and mix with the spring onions, beansprouts, carrots and green pepper.

Mix all the remaining ingredients in a cup and pour over the salad. Toss and serve.

BEANSPROUT SALAD WITH FETA CHEESE   [A]

In Greece no lettuce and tomato salad is complete without a sprinkling of crumbled Feta cheese, and the idea works just as well with this salad.

6 oz/175 g Chinese beansprouts
½ small iceberg lettuce, shredded
12 small black olives
2 tablespoons salted peanuts
1 tablespoon olive oil
1 tablespoon lemon juice
4 oz/100 g Feta cheese, crumbled
pinch dried oregano
freshly ground black pepper

Toss the beansprouts in a bowl with the shredded lettuce. Sprinkle with olives and nuts.

Mix the olive oil and lemon juice and pour over the top. Next sprinkle with Feta cheese and then with oregano and black pepper.

NOVEMBER

'There was an Old Person of Bangor,
Whose face was distorted with anger,
He tore off his boots and subsisted on roots,
That borascible person of Bangor.'

Edward Lear (1812—1888)

Chicory
Kohlrabi
Swede
Okra

CHICORY

This is the endive of Continental recipes. At one time it was known as 'succory' and sometimes as *witloof* — Dutch for white leaf. In the US it is called French or Belgian endive or witloof-chicory.

Availability: September to February.

Buying Guide: Look for conical specimens with crisp, white, tightly packed leaves. Avoid those with green tips to the leaves. They are getting old.

Storage: Keep for a day or two in the salad compartment of the fridge.

Preparation: Wash well and leave whole to cook. Divide into leaves or slice for salads.

Basic Cooking: Blanch in boiling water with a little lemon juice for 5 minutes and drain. Steam in a very little lemon water and serve with sauce, or braise in butter or a little stock or wine. Wrap in ham and bake in a cheese sauce.

CHICORY WINTER SALAD   [M]

I find that this salad makes a real midday meal in itself. But if you think you will be hungry, add a wholemeal roll and butter, or some cold savoury rice.

4 oz/100 g frozen peas
salt
4 heads chicory, sliced
3 hard-boiled eggs, chopped
4 oz/100 g Cheddar cheese, diced
black pepper
2 tablespoons mayonnaise
1 teaspoon lemon juice
pinch dried mixed herbs
1 bunch watercress

Cook the peas in lightly salted boiling water for 8 minutes. Drain and rinse under the cold tap. Leave to cool in a sieve.

Mix all the remaining ingredients together except the watercress. Stir the peas into the chicory mixture and add the lemon mayonnaise. Toss well together and pile into the centre of a serving dish. Surround with sprigs of watercress.

CHICORY ARDENNAISE [A]

This is a variation on the Belgian classic of braised chicory. Add a light cheese sauce for a good supper dish.

1 oz/25 g butter
4 large heads chicory
salt and black pepper
1 oz/25 g streaky bacon, diced
1 oz/25 g cooked ham, diced

Melt the butter in a heavy-based saucepan and arrange the whole heads of chicory in the bottom. Season and cover the pan with foil, then with a lid. Cook over a very low heat for 20 minutes, shaking the pan from time to time.

Fry the bacon in its own fat in a non-stick frying pan and then add the ham. Sprinkle the mixture over the chicory, re-cover and continue cooking for a further 10—15 minutes until the chicory is tender.

CHICORY SALAD WITH ORANGES [A]

This makes a refreshing salad to serve between courses.

2 oranges, peeled and sliced
2 heads chicory
2 tablespoons olive oil
freshly ground black pepper

Pile the orange slices into the centre of a round serving plate. Divide the chicory into leaves and arrange them in a star shape around the orange. Drizzle with oil and sprinkle with black pepper.

CHICORY SALAD WITH GRAPEFRUIT [A]

As a variation of the above recipe, use 1 grapefruit in place of the oranges.

KOHLRABI

This is a hybrid member of the cabbage family. The leaves may be eaten like spinach but it is usually the swollen base stem which is used. It tastes a little like a cabbagey turnip and looks rather like a mauve turnip with shoots.

It was introduced from Italy into Germany in the middle of the sixteenth century. France has cultivated it for several hundred years, but it is not at all well known in this country.

Availability: October to March.

Buying Guide: Look for small young specimens for they toughen with age. Avoid any which are wizened or have worm holes.

Storage: Keep for a day or two in the salad compartment of the fridge.

Preparation: Wash and cook whole. Very young kohlrabi may be used in salads tossed in lemon juice.

Basic Cooking: Steam in a very little salted water for about 30 minutes until tender. Drain, peel and slice. Serve with butter or a white sauce. Purée with butter and milk or other vegetables. Bake au gratin or use for fritters. Use cold in salads with a mayonnaise or vinaigrette dressing.

GRATIN OF KOHLRABI [S]

This dish makes a very unusual starter, or it may be served as a vegetable accompaniment to a casserole or roast.

4 kohlrabi, peeled and sliced
salt and black pepper
¼ pint/150 ml double cream
2 egg yolks

Cook the kohlrabi in a very little salted boiling water until just tender. Drain, retaining the cooking liquor. Place in four individual heatproof dishes and keep warm.

Bring the cooking liquor to the boil again and continue boiling until it is reduced to about 3 tablespoonfuls. Lightly whisk the cream and whisk in the egg yolks. Pour this mixture into the vegetable liquid and heat gently, whisking all the time. Do not allow the mixture to boil.

When the mixture begins to thicken a little, pour it over the kohlrabi and place under a hot grill until a thin golden skin forms on the surface. Serve at once.

KOHLRABI POLONAISE   [A]

This dressing is perhaps more often served with cauliflower, but it works just as effectively with kohlrabi.

1 lb/450 g kohlrabi
1 oz/50 g butter
2 hard-boiled egg yolks
1 tablespoon freshly chopped parsley
2 tablespoons fresh breadcrumbs

Cook the kohlrabi in a steamer or in a little salted boiling water until tender. Drain well and dice. Sauté in half the butter and then spoon into a warmed serving dish.

Rub the egg yolks through a sieve and sprinkle over the kohlrabi with the parsley. Fry the breadcrumbs in the remaining butter until well browned and sprinkle over the top of the dish. Serve at once.

SPECIAL TIP. Purée as on page 14 and serve with roast or grilled meats. Alternatively, use instead of Parsnip Rémoulade on page 25 and serve with cold meats and salad.

SWEDE

Swede is an abbreviation of Swedish turnip. In Scotland and northern England they are known just as turnips or 'neeps'.

Although they have been known in northern Europe for centuries it was not until the eighteenth century that swedes came to England from Sweden. It was soon found they they could withstand the cold winters in northern parts of the country, and in Scotland they were widely grown as cattle fodder.

By the nineteenth century people were starting to eat them and they appeared in mutton stews and in Cornish pasties. Today they are more often served mashed with butter and, as such, are the traditional accompaniment to the Burns Night haggis in Scotland.

Availability: September to May.

Buying Guide: Avoid over-large swedes which may be woody in the centre.

Storage: Keep in a cool, dry airy place for a few days.

Preparation: Peel thinly and slice or dice. Grate for salads.

Basic Cooking: Boil or steam in a little salted water. Purée with butter or mix with mashed potatoes. Use as a topping for shepherds' pie. Cut into sticks and stir-fry with other vegetables or slice and braise in the oven. They can also be added sparingly to soups and stews.

SWEDE SOUP WITH FRIED CROÛTONS [S]

New young turnips at the beginning of the season can also be used for this recipe. If liked the tops can be included. This gives the soup a pretty pale green colour.

1 onion, sliced
1 leek, sliced (if available)
3 oz/75 g butter
1 tablespoon cooking oil
1 lb/450 g swede, peeled and diced
1 large potato, peeled and diced
2 pints/1.2 litres chicken stock
salt and black pepper
2 large slices white bread
3 tablespoons double cream

Gently fry the onion and leek in 1 oz/25 g of the butter and the cooking oil. After a minute or two add the rest of the vegetables and continue cooking gently for another 2—3 minutes.

Pour on the stock and add the seasoning. Bring the soup to the boil and simmer for 30 minutes until the vegetables are tender.

Meanwhile fry the bread in the rest of the butter until crisp and golden on both sides. Drain on kitchen paper and cut into small dice. When the soup is cooked, purée in a blender and sieve. Reheat and stir in the cream. Serve sprinkled with croûtons.

SWEDE AND POTATO PIE   [M]

This dish makes a very good supper dish served with buttered broccoli or spring greens.

2 lb/1 kg swede, peeled and sliced
1 lb/450 g potatoes, peeled and sliced
2 oz/50 g butter
2 tablespoons single cream
salt and pepper
4 oz/100 g Cheddar cheese, grated
2 oz/50 g wholemeal breadcrumbs

Cover the swede with water and bring to the boil. Cook for 5 minutes and add the potatoes. Cover again and continue cooking for 10—15 minutes until both vegetables are tender.

Drain very well and then mash the two vegetables together. Beat in the butter, cream and seasonings and spoon into a buttered casserole dish.

Mix the cheese and breadcrumbs and pile up on the top. Bake at 200°C/400°F/Gas 6 for 20—30 minutes until crisp and golden on top.

SWEDE WITH ONIONS AND GARLIC   [A]

This method of dealing with swede really turns the rather humble vegetable into a delicious dish. Serve with steak or grilled chops.

8 oz/225 g onions, sliced
2 tablespoons cooking oil
1 lb/450 g swede, peeled and cut into thin sticks
1 clove garlic, crushed
½ oz/15 g plain flour
¼ pint/150 ml chicken stock
¼ pint/150 ml milk

salt and pepper
2 tablespoons freshly chopped parsley

Fry the onion in the cooking oil for 1 minute and then add the swede sticks and garlic. Continue frying gently over a low heat for about 30 minutes until the vegetables are tender. Stir from time to time.

Add the flour and gradually add the chicken stock and milk, stirring all the time. Bring the mixture to the boil and season. Continue cooking for about 15 minutes until the liquid has reduced to about a third of its original volume. Turn into a dish and serve sprinkled with chopped parsley.

SPICED SWEDE   [A]

Parsley can be substituted for the fresh coriander but the result will not be quite the same.

2 tablespoons cooking oil
1 in/2.5 cm piece of root ginger, peeled and grated
4 tomatoes, peeled and chopped
1 tablespoon ground coriander
½ teaspoon turmeric
salt and pepper
1 lb/450 g swede, peeled and cut into thin sticks
2 tablespoons freshly chopped green coriander
1 tablespoon freshly chopped mint

Heat the cooking oil in a pan and add the ginger and tomatoes. Cook gently for 2—3 minutes. Add the spices and seasoning and stir well.

Add the swede and fresh herbs and cook for about 30 minutes until the swede is tender, stirring from time to time. Add a little water if the mixture shows signs of drying up.

SPICED SWEDE WITH CARROTS   [A]

As a variation of the above, use 8 oz/225 g carrots, peeled and cut into sticks, in place of half the swede. Continue as above.

OKRA

This vegetable is also known as ladies' fingers. It is a mucilaginous aromatic bean. It grows in most tropical countries and is used extensively in African, Middle Eastern and American cooking. It is also used in India and South East Asia. In America no gumbo would be complete without it.

It is important not to damage the bean pod during preparation or water will get in and the result with be rather slimy. Soaking in acidulated water can reduce the mucilage.

Availability: All the year round.

Buying Guide: Choose firm specimens with a good colour. Avoid limp okra with brown patches.

Storage: Use as soon as possible after purchase. Keep in the salad drawer of the fridge until needed.

Preparation: Trim the stalks but do not cut into the okra pod itself. Wash and, for a less gelatinous end result, soak for an hour in water acidulated with 2–3 tablespoons vinegar.

Basic Cooking: Boil in salted water for 9–12 minutes depending on size. Serve with butter and spices such as cumin or coriander. Parboil and braise for 30 minutes or cook with tomatoes and onions and eat hot or cold.

OKRA IRAQI-STYLE   [A]

Okra is one of the basic vegetables of Iraq and is used in all kinds of dishes from soups to stews. This dish is good served with roast and grilled meats or with other spicy dishes.

1 lb/450 g okra
1 large onion, sliced
1 clove garlic, chopped
1 tablespoon olive oil
4 tomatoes, peeled and chopped
½ teaspoon ground coriander
¼ teaspoon turmeric
salt and freshly ground black pepper
juice of ½ lemon

Cut the stems off the okra taking care not to cut into the main body of the vegetable. Fry the onion and garlic in the olive oil until very lightly browned. Add the okra and gently fry with the onions for a minute or two.

Add all the remaining ingredients, and bring to the boil. Cover and simmer for about 20—30 minutes until the okra is tender. Take care not to overcook or the okra will go mushy.

CHICKEN GUMBO   [M]

This is a version of the traditional Louisiana gumbo which uses chicken instead of shellfish. Gumbos always include okra. Indeed in some French-speaking Caribbean countries okra itself is called gumbo.

2 rashers bacon, diced
2 onions, chopped
2 sticks celery, chopped
1 small green pepper, seeded and chopped
1 oz/25 g butter
4 oz/100 g sweetcorn
4 medium tomatoes, chopped
8 oz/225 g okra, trimmed
½ pint/300 ml chicken stock
a few drops Tabasco sauce
salt and black pepper
1 small roasted chicken
8 oz/225 g rice

Gently fry the bacon, onion, celery and green pepper in the butter, stirring from time to time. Do not allow the vegetables to brown. Place the sweetcorn, tomatoes and okra in a saucepan with the chicken stock and bring to the boil. Add the fried vegetables, Tabasco and seasoning and continue boiling for 15 minutes.

Remove the cooked chicken meat from the bones and cut into chunks. Cook the rice in ¾ pint/450 ml salted boiling water for 15 minutes until all the liquid has disappeared and the rice is tender. Add the chicken to the gumbo mixture and heat through.

Press the rice into four cups and turn out into the centre of four large heated soup bowls. Spoon the gumbo round the outside and serve at once.

DRY-FRIED OKRA WITH COUSCOUS [A]

Contrary to the usual practice, the okra here is sliced. The gelatinous liquid which comes from the okra is taken up by the couscous and the end result is deliciously dry and crisp.

12 oz/350 g okra, trimmed and sliced
½ green pepper, seeded and thinly sliced
½ red pepper, seeded and thinly sliced
4 oz/100 g couscous, or medium cornmeal or polenta
salt and pepper
3 tablespoons cooking oil

Toss okra, peppers and couscous in a bowl and ensure an even mix. Heat the oil in a frying pan and add the okra mixture, then cook over a medium heat for 10–12 minutes, stirring frequently. Serve at once.

DECEMBER

'At Christmas I no more desire a rose
Than wish a snow in May's new-fangled mirth,
But like each thing that is in season grows.'

Love's Labour Lost, William Shakespeare (1564—1616)

Brussels Sprouts
Salsify and Scorzonera
Cauliflower
Sweet Potatoes and Yams

BRUSSELS SPROUTS

Sixteenth-century fruit and vegetable cultivation was at a much more advanced stage in the low countries of Belgium and Holland than it was in Britain. One of the vegetables being developed around that time was the Brussels sprout, and it was soon exported along with other garden produce to the UK.

Sprouts are a member of the cabbage family and they originated from the wild cabbage. Around Brussels any sprouts smaller than a small plum are sneered at, whereas in France the preference is for very tiny sprouts. The UK taste is somewhere in the middle, though smaller more delicate varieties are appearing.

In the past sprouts were sometimes served with red cabbage, sometimes with grapes and other fruit. They were also puréed and mixed with cream and chestnut purée, and this is now becoming popular again.

Availability: September to March.

Buying Guide: Sprouts should be fresh with tightly packed leaves. Avoid any which are turning yellow or which are very large and open. Sprout tops are also available and these look rather like small spring greens but with a little more of a heart. They have a similar flavour to sprouts and should be bright in colour and not at all limp.

Storage: Eat as soon as possible after purchase. Wash, trim and store in a polythene container in the fridge until needed.

Preparation: Wash well and remove any tough or dirty outer leaves. Split the stalks of larger sprouts. Shred for use in salads.

Basic Cooking: Boil or steam in a very little salted water. Drain and toss in butter with a pinch of nutmeg or in soured cream. Parboil and braise in stock on their own or with whole chestnuts. Slice cooked sprouts and use in Bubble and Squeak.

BRUSSELS SPROUT AND CHESTNUT SOUP   [S]

1 onion, chopped
1 tablespoon cooking oil
2 fl. oz/50 ml dry sherry
1 lb/450 g Brussels sprouts, sliced
4 oz/100 g chestnuts, shelled and sliced or 3 oz/75 g whole canned
    chestnuts, unsweetened
½ pint/300 ml milk
1 pint/600 ml chicken stock
salt and black pepper
4 tablespoons single cream

Fry the onion in cooking oil until it turns translucent. Add the
sherry and bring to the boil. Add all the remaining ingredients
except the cream and return to the boil. Simmer for 20 minutes
until the vegetables and chestnuts are tender.

Purée in a blender or sieve. Reheat and serve with a swirl of
cream in each dish.

BRUSSELS SPROUTS WITH BREADCRUMBS   [A]

Variations on this simple but effective recipe include a little cinnamon or allspice shaken into the breadcrumbs.

1 lb/450 g Brussels sprouts, washed and trimmed
salt
2 oz/50 g butter
3 oz/75 g fresh breadcrumbs

Cook the sprouts in a little salted boiling water until just tender.
Melt the butter in a frying pan and fry the breadcrumbs until
well browned. Add the well-drained sprouts and stir until they are
coated with breadcrumbs. Turn into a warmed serving dish.

BRUSSELS SPROUTS MILANAISE   [A]

Almost any vegetable can be given this classic Italian treatment, but it seems particularly to bring out the flavour of Brussels sprouts. Make sure that you do not overcook them to start with.

1 lb/450 g Brussels sprouts, washed and trimmed
2 oz/50 g butter
3 oz/75 g cheese, grated
freshly ground black pepper

Cook the sprouts in a little lightly salted boiling water, or steam in a steamer until tender. Drain well and sauté in half the butter until very lightly browned.

Sprinkle the base of a buttered heatproof dish with half the cheese. Spoon in the sprouts and sprinkle with black pepper. Next add the remainder of the cheese and leave in a warm place until the cheese begins to melt.

Heat the remaining butter in a small saucepan until it begins to turn brown and pour over the sprouts, leaving the sediment behind in the pan. Serve at once.

BRUSSELS SPROUTS AND CARROT SALAD   [A]

Brussels sprouts, although usually served hot, make an excellent base for a winter salad.

1 lb/450 g Brussels sprouts
1 tablespoon finely chopped onion
2 medium carrots, grated
2 tablespoons sultanas
4 tablespoons olive oil
1 tablespoon wine vinegar
salt and pepper

Prepare the sprouts, then remove a slice from the base of each. Shred coarsely and mix with the onion, carrot and sultanas. Mix together the remaining ingredients to make a dressing and stir in enough to moisten the vegetables.

SALSIFY AND SCORZONERA

Salsify, a long white-rooted vegetable, was known in some parts as the 'vegetable oyster' because of the faint sea-flavour of its roots. A very similar plant is scorzonera. The only real difference is that these roots are black in colour.

These are vegetables which are much more popular on the Continent than in the UK. However, it is possible to find either or both in some specialist greengrocers.

Availability: October to late spring.

Buying Guide: Look for regular-shaped tapered roots. Avoid anything damaged or discoloured or which is shrivelled-looking.

Storage: Keep in a cool, dry place for a day or two.

Preparation: Scrape rather than peel the roots and drop immediately into salted water containing a little lemon juice. This helps to prevent them discolouring.

Basic Cooking: Boil whole or in 3 in/7.5 cm lengths for 40 minutes and serve tossed in butter flavoured with fresh herbs. Or boil for 30 minutes and finish off in butter or milk. If the latter use the cooking liquor to make a cream or cheese sauce. Use parboiled salsify for fritters or to shallow-fry. Use cold cooked salsify as a starter with vinaigrette or in salads with other vegetables.

VEGETABLE OYSTER SOUP [S]

This soup has a really delicate flavour.

1 tablespoon plain flour
hot water
1 lb/450 g salsify roots
a little lemon juice
3 tablespoons single cream
1 oz/25 g butter
salt and pepper

Mix the flour with a little hot water to form a smooth cream.

Peel and grate the salsify and place in a saucepan. Just cover with water — about 1½ pints/850 ml — and add the lemon juice and flour/water mixture. Bring to the boil and simmer for 40 minutes until tender.

Liquidise or rub through a sieve. Whisk in the cream and butter and season to taste. Bring to the boil and serve.

SALSIFY WITH TOMATOES AND HERBS [A]

Add a little garlic, if you like it, to this Mediterranean way with salsify. But take care or you will overwhelm the flavour of the vegetable itself.

12 oz/350 g cooked salsify, cut into lengths
1 oz/25 g butter
2 tablespoons freshly chopped parsley
1 tablespoon freshly chopped chives
4 tomatoes, peeled, seeded and chopped
2 tablespoons tomato juice
salt and black pepper

Fry the salsify in butter until lightly browned and then add the herbs and tomatoes. Cook for another minute or so and then add the tomato juice and seasonings.

Bring to the boil and cook for 5 minutes. Serve sprinkled with a little more fresh parsley.

SALSIFY SALAD WITH MANGETOUT [A]

Both the salsify and the mangetout have very delicate flavours and for the very best results are served without any additional flavourings.

6 oz/175 g mangetout
8 oz/225 g cooked salsify
2 tablespoons salad oil
2 teaspoons wine vinegar
salt
freshly ground black pepper

Blanch the mangetout in boiling water for 1 minute, drain and refresh in cold water. Drain again and cut diagonally, with scissors, into strips. Cut the cooked salsify into sticks and mix with the mangetout and place in a serving dish.

Mix all the remaining ingredients together and pour over the vegetables. Chill for 30 minutes and serve.

CAULIFLOWER

Cauliflowers have along history but they were only introduced into the UK in Elizabethan times when they were a high-priced luxury. Cauliflowers were available only to the wealthy and they used to enjoy them served in rich creamy sauces. Cauliflower cheese is probably the modern equivalent of these dishes.

Nowadays, cauliflowers are grown by the million and even though they can still be quite expensive they are popular with almost everyone.

Availability: All the year round.

Buying Guide: Avoid loose-packed, woolly or damaged heads. Yellow heads do not mean a loss of flavour and as these specimens should be sold at a cheaper rate they are good for soups or for dishes where the florets will be disguised in some way. The base of the stalk should be clean and white.

Storage: Eat as soon as possible after purchase. Keep wrapped in clingfilm or foil in the salad drawer of the fridge.

Preparation: Trim leaves and stalks and wash well. Cook whole or cut into portions. Separate into small florets or chop for use in salads and as crudités.

Basic Cooking: Steam, stalk side down, in a very little salted boiling water for about 12–15 minutes. Take care not to overcook or it will go mushy. Serve with a sauce or a topping of fried breadcrumbs and other flavourings. Par-boil and use for egg and breadcrumb fritters. Serve with tartare sauce.

CREAM OF CAULIFLOWER AND MUSTARD SOUP   [S]

This is a variation on the classic French soup. Crème Dubarry. For the latter simply leave out the French mustard.

1 oz/25 g butter
1 small onion, sliced
1 head cauliflower, cut into pieces
3 fl. oz/75 ml dry sherry
1 tablespoon French mustard
1½ pints/900 ml vegetable stock or water

½ teaspoon sugar
salt and pepper
4 tablespoons single cream
mustard and cress

Melt the butter in a large pan and fry the onion for 3—4 minutes until lightly browned. Add the cauliflower and continue cooking for a minute or two. Pour on the sherry and bring to the boil. Add all the remaining ingredients except the cream and mustard and cress.

Return to the boil. Reduce the heat, cover and simmer for about 30—40 minutes until the cauliflower is tender. Blend or sieve. Reheat and serve garnished with a swirl of cream and a little mustard and cress.

CAULIFLOWER WITH ALMONDS [A]

This is another French idea. I tried it while on holiday there and my guests were extremely complimentary.

1 cauliflower
salt
2 oz/50 g flaked almonds
1 tablespoon raisins
2 oz/50 g butter

Cook the cauliflower stem side down in a very little lightly salted water until almost tender. Drain, cut into florets and arrange in a serving dish. Keep warm.

Toast the flaked almonds and raisins under the grill. Melt the butter in a pan and pour off the clear liquid into another pan. Add the toasted almonds and raisins and reheat. Pour over the cauliflower and serve at once.

WINTER SALAD [A]

Cauliflower is very good eaten raw. Try small florets as dippers for Guacamole (page 32), or use them in this crunchy winter salad.

½ cauliflower, cut into small florets
1 x 7 oz/200 g can red pimentos, drained and finely chopped
3 in/7.5 cm cucumber, diced
1 green apple, cored and diced

1 tablespoon flaked almonds
3 tablespoons salad oil
1 tablespoon white wine vinegar

Place all the ingredients except the oil and vinegar in a bowl and toss lightly together.

Mix the oil and vinegar and pour over the top. Chill for 30 minutes. Toss again and serve.

PICKLED CAULIFLOWER [A]

This is really a recipe to try in the summer when the sun may be out for long enough to pickle the cauliflower outside. But cauliflower is more likely to be cheap at this time of the year, so use the airing cupboard if you have one. It makes enough to fill 2 x 1 lb/450 g jars.

1 small cauliflower, cut into florets
7 fl. oz/200 ml white wine vinegar
juice of ½ lemon
1½ tablespoons honey
½ teaspoon fresh root ginger, peeled and grated
½ teaspoon mustard seeds
2 teaspoons salt

Place all the ingredients in a jar and shake well together. Leave in the sun or in a warm place and shake up twice a day. It will be ready to eat after two weeks but will keep for longer.

SWEET POTATOES AND YAMS

Originating in the Americas these vegetables have grown in popularity in the UK in recent years and are now available in most supermarkets.

When Columbus brought sweet potatoes back from one of his early trips to the New World he described them as looking like yams — with which Europe was already familiar — and tasting like a chestnut. The potatoes flourished in the warm soils of Spain and Portugal and in the sixteenth century they were called Spanish Potatoes. Drake brought samples to the UK around 1560 and they were served with roast beef in place of parsnips or turnips.

Sweet potatoes look rather like reddish potatoes with thick skins. They have an orange coloured flesh and a sweet flavour. Yams are another root vegetable from the West Indies. They have a dark skin and are larger and less sweet than sweet potatoes but they can both be used in much the same ways as British potatoes.

Availability: All the year round.

Buying Guide: Choose firm specimens with little or no damage.

Storage: Keep in a cool, dark, airy place for a week or so.

Preparation: Cook in their skins or peel and slice or dice. Drop yams into water with lemon juice to prevent discolouring.

Basic Cooking: Bake whole in their skins or par-boil for 10 minutes and roast like ordinary potatoes. Alternatively boil and mash with butter and other flavourings such as fresh herbs, spices or orange juice. Slice and bake in the oven with a cheese topping or with other vegetables.

SPICED YAMS   [A]

Go easy on the red chilli peppers if you are not too keen on 'hot' food. This recipe comes from Jamaica where they are very fond of really hot peppers.

1½ lb/700 g yams, peeled and cubed
a little lemon juice
1 onion, finely chopped
1 tablespoon cooking oil
3 red chilli peppers, seeded and chopped
½ teaspoon allspice
pinch nutmeg
salt and pepper

Cook the yams with the lemon juice in salted boiling water for about 15 minutes until tender. Drain well.

Meanwhile fry the onion in cooking oil until lightly browned. Add all the remaining ingredients and the yams. Fry for 3–4 minutes, turning from time to time.

SWEET POTATO CASSEROLE [A]

Serve this American speciality with fried chicken and salad.

4 small sweet potatoes, washed
2 oz/50 g butter
1 oz/25 g brown sugar
salt
1 tablespoon sherry
½ x 8 oz/225 g can pineapple slices, drained and chopped
¼ teaspoon grated nutmeg
1 oz/25 g raisins

Bake the sweet potatoes at 190°C/375°F/Gas 5 for about an hour until tender. Cut off the tops, scoop out the flesh and mash with a fork.

Place the butter, sugar, salt and sherry in a saucepan and heat gently, stirring all the time. When the sugar has dissolved and the butter melted, add the pineapple, nutmeg and raisins and mix with the mashed potatoes.

Pile the mixture back into the potato skins and return to the oven and bake for a further 10 minutes.

HAWAIIAN SWEET POTATOES

In Hawaii this may be served with the meat course but I think that in the UK it is better suited to be a dessert.

1 lb/450 g sweet potatoes
1 banana, peeled and diced
1 tablespoon brown sugar
juice of ½ grapefruit
2 tablespoons desiccated coconut

Boil the sweet potatoes in their jackets for about 1 hour, 20 minutes until tender. Leave to cool and then peel and dice. Mix with the banana and spoon into a casserole dish.

Dissolve the sugar in the grapefruit juice, warming if necessary, and pour over the sweet potato and banana.

Bake at 190°C/375°F/Gas 5 for 30 minutes. Sprinkle the coconut over the top and finish off under the grill to lightly brown.

SPECIAL TIP. Candied Sweet Potatoes, the traditional American accompaniment to turkey for Thanksgiving Day, is made by mixing 1 lb/450 g diced cooked sweet potatoes with 3 oz/75 g muscovado sugar, a little grated lemon rind, 1 tablespoon lemon juice and ½ oz/15 g melted butter. Bake in an ovenproof dish at 190°C/375°F/ Gas 5 for 35 minutes.

INDEX